# LEVERS

## THE FRAMEWORK FOR BUILDING REPEATABILITY INTO YOUR BUSINESS

# AMOS SCHWARTZFARB

### AND

# TREVOR BOEHM

### WITH CODY SIMMS AND TROY HENIKOFF

**LIONCREST**
PUBLISHING

LEVERS

*The Framework for Building Repeatability into Your Business*

ISBN    978-1-5445-1981-4   *Hardcover*
           978-1-5445-1980-7   *Paperback*
           978-1-5445-1979-1   *Ebook*

*To every person who has ever tried to build a business from day zero. This is hard and you are amazing!*

# CONTENTS

# INTRODUCTION

What makes some companies work and others not?

Not just the unicorn-status kind of work. We mean work in the fundamental kind of way—where the company is solving real problems for customers and seeing repeatable, sustainable growth. Where things are working for you, where the business almost seems to run on its own. Where, as the operator, you have such a keen understanding of how your business works that it's almost as if you have a crystal ball into the future. It's when you can call your next shot in the business, and then it actually happens.

When we (Amos Schwartzfarb and Trevor Boehm) first started working together, we would talk about this question: Considering the companies you've worked with, what is the difference between those that succeeded and those that failed?

Amos had a simple answer: "With every company that I've been a part of that worked, I could see in advance how we were going to succeed before we did."

His secret was that he could visualize not just what the business could become, but also how it could get there. In other words, he had a data-driven model for how the business worked. It was like he was seeing the business as one big machine, with a series of levers that, if pulled in the right way and in the right order, would spit out cash as predictably as an ATM.

We've been thinking and acting according to these terms with our own companies and with the companies we've invested in now for over a decade. And we've seen, even if only intuitively, every successful serial entrepreneur we respect does the same. They don't blindly trust their gut and launch into some massive undertaking or chase an industry or venture capital (VC) trend, accruing gigantic risk in hopes of cashing in on some technological or hype wave. Instead, they start with a core belief about whom they want to serve, what that person needs, and why they need it. Then, action by action, they start piecing together a theory for how they could capture value while serving them, using data to test and expand their understanding every step along the way. Put simply, they identify the levers of control in their business, and then they move those levers.

## THE FRAMEWORK FOR BUILDING REPEATABILITY IN YOUR BUSINESS

The goal of this book is to take that process of finding the levers and creating repeatability in your business—what we're convinced every successful entrepreneur does to reach his or her success—and make it a playbook for anyone. We've laid it out as a simple framework that any entrepreneur can use, whether they're just getting started or are millions of dollars—or hours, or scars—in.

We wrote this book to take business builders of all kinds out of the world of constant hustle and uncertainty into a world of clarity and control. We don't promise that if you use this process you will have a successful business. We do believe that this process will give you the shortest path to finding a plan to massively increase the likelihood you'll succeed, as well as the chance to execute on that plan.

The framework is a set of five tools, and behind those tools are five fundamental questions about your business. They are:

1. Who is my customer, what are they buying, and why?
2. How do I create value and ultimately revenue?
3. What do I do now and next?
4. Is what I'm doing working?
5. What's my plan?

We're by far not the first people to think up or ask these questions. The insight of this process and the book is to organize these questions into a single framework, laid out in the language of data. Once you have all these pieces, you'll begin to think of your business as one cohesive model. In Chapter 5, we'll demonstrate the full manifestation of that thinking as we guide you through building and using a working financial model to run your business.

We have zero expectations that any company will figure it all out on the first try. Some companies may even take years. Similarly, you should fully expect that finding the answers to these questions will take a very long time. Remember, this isn't a recipe. It's a manual on how to cook so you can start making *your own* recipes.

## WHO WE ARE

Amos and Trevor are the main authors of this book with collaboration from two additional contributors: Cody Simms (who co-wrote Chapter 3 and the appendix) and Troy Henikoff (who wrote Chapter 5).

At our cores, each of the authors in this book is a business builder. We've been leading and investing in companies for decades.

We have grown companies to $100M+ in revenue and collectively more than a billion in acquisitions, served in executive roles with other businesses who were doing billions in revenue, and have been on the founding team of, invested in, or advised hundreds (likely thousands) of early-stage startups and small businesses, including as a part of the global accelerator Techstars, Northwestern University's Kellogg School of Business, and through our own funds.

Most of us have also been around the block a few times. We've been in key roles at companies through every boom and bust cycle in the tech industry and the economy generally for the last twenty-five years.

Each writer brings a unique set of functional expertise that spans sales, products, operations, and finance. Our vision for this book is to give you the feeling of having an entire veteran C-suite working on your business, right alongside you.

## WHY YOU SHOULD READ THIS BOOK

So why read this book? Because it will give you the five most important foundational elements for finding repeatability in your business along with actionable frameworks so that you can build the biggest, most meaningful, and longest-term business possible.

More specifically, over the course of the coming chapters, our goal is to provide you with a progressive foundation to build repeatability in every part of your business so that you can control your own outcome.

*Levers* is designed to bridge the gap between tactics and vision for entrepreneurs, aligning your team toward a compelling, metrics-driven strategy. If you read this book and put in the work the exercises require, you'll start to see a few major things change.

First, as a team, you'll start to *say the same things*.

The book is designed to help you create your own shared language for who your customer is, how you create value, and your plan for growing the business. Even midway through the process, you should start to hear a major shift in the ways you talk about your business as a team, and more importantly, everyone will be on the same page.

Second, you will start to *know what's working, what's not working, and why*.

The power of a metrics-driven business is its ability to tell you, with a strong degree of confidence, whether all that effort you're putting into the business actually matters. As you identify and refine things you need to prove in your business and how you'll measure and track progress, you will become a master at learning in your business.

Third, you will feel *less out of control.*

Let's face it, building a company is painful. There are simply too many things that can go wrong—customers leave, employees quit (or you shouldn't have hired them in the first place), markets swing—and that's not accounting for all the ways our personal and work lives inevitably crash into each other when we're pouring ourselves into a thing we care deeply about. The ultimate outcome of this book is to give you back control in your business by having a deep, data-driven understanding of how it actually works.

There are plenty of great resources that help entrepreneurs rely on external validation (fundraising, pitching, etc.) for their success. Our goal is to help you build real, repeatable value in your business that you can control. This is the book for companies who aren't interested in just playing the VC game or leaving their success to chance, but who want the freedom that comes from being able to create their own future.

It's our belief that these concepts are essential for any business of any kind regardless of who your customers are or what industry you are in. We've presented them in the order that we believe makes the most sense. Although it's possible for them to stand alone, the sum is more than its parts. The concepts move from simple to complex, from fundamental to operational. If you jump into one without really understanding what comes before it, you risk finding yourself missing something fundamental about your business.

And this isn't just reading; it's also doing. Every chapter is real work. Sure, you can just read it and get the gist, but we also give you the tools to turn theory into practice.

## THE BIG VISION

Our ultimate aim of this book is to create a new generation of business builders who control their own destinies—who wake up every day telling themselves, "I can't believe I get to do this for a living!"

Running a company can be one of the greatest experiences—and privileges—in life. We want every entrepreneur to deeply understand how to move their business forward and then be free to build the world they imagine. Whether that world is millions of transformed customers, a system free from injustice, or just more time with your family, the path to it starts with knowing the levers of control in your business.

Good luck! We look forward to seeing how you turn your vision into a reality. And if you are looking for more hands-on help, you can go to leversbook.com or email us at apply@leversbook.com.

# CHAPTER 1

# W3

## (BY AMOS SCHWARTZFARB)

*Who is my customer? What are they*
*buying? Why are they buying it?*

I met Char Hu, CEO of The Helper Bees, in September 2015. With a PhD in biophysics, in 2010, he had started a group of assisted living residences for those afflicted by Alzheimer's and dementia. He came to me because he had an idea for helping aging adults stay in their homes instead of moving to assisted living. He applied to join Techstars Austin before he even had a website, much less a product. But he did have an incredible amount of industry expertise.

Char and his team launched The Helper Bees as a marketplace for connecting aging adults with neighbors in their community who could help them with tasks around the house. You might think that a business like this would market to aging adults since that's whom they served. But early on, they discovered more often than not, it wasn't the aging adult who was looking for the help. It was their children. Daughters and daughters-in-law, to be exact. So The Helper Bees started marketing to daughters and daughters-in-law in their mid-forties and fifties, and their growth exploded.

Fast-forward three years. Char and the team began looking for ways to expand even faster. They noticed that when you serve aging adults, there is another group you will inevitability run across: insurance companies. And insurance companies, like forty-seven-year-old daughters, wanted to keep aging adults in their homes longer, too (albeit for different reasons). So they shifted their focus and started to target insurance companies.

Fast-forward to 2020. The Helper Bees had seen the kind of growth only a few very lucky companies ever get to see.

For Char and The Helper Bees, what started as a service for aging adults also became a service for daughters and, eventually, a service for some of the country's biggest insurance companies. Char knew to start with three core questions: *Who? What?* and *Why?* And more so, Char knew he had to keep answering these questions over and over as the business continued to grow and scale.

## WHAT IS W3?

W3 stands for the three first and most important questions you need to answer to validate whether your business is even a good idea and if it has any chance of being successful.[1] W3 is the

---

1   For those of you who have read *Sell More Faster*, much of what is in this chapter will be familiar. The content is based off that book's Chapter 1, though it's in a different context. If you've read that chapter, this exercise may move a bit faster for you than if it's your first time through. However, I still urge you to take the time to do the work (or redo it) in order to get the most out of the chapters to come. It'll also be a great opportunity to test and reevaluate your current theories.

entire reason that you decided to build your business to begin with, and it's the guiding light that will keep you growing, learning, and innovating so you can bring value to a group of people while also making money and building a phenomenal business.

The three simple questions are:

- **Who** do you believe your customer is or will be?
- **What** does your customer buy from you (not what you sell to them)?
- **Why** does your customer buy your product (or why do you think they will)?

Simple, right? But not easy to figure out, and even harder to collect the data to prove that you are right. Until you prove your W3 theories are right—by doing the work of talking to customers, testing concepts, collecting data, analyzing the data, getting more customers, and then doing it all over again—you will not be on the path to reaching repeatability or your maximum potential.

The reality is, this theorizing and testing never stops. Even when you have proven it for where you are, if you want to continue to grow and innovate and remain a viable business, you need to do this work all the time, always questioning if and how it's changing. Your answers will continue to evolve, just as the tools and technology around us are always changing.

## A FEW ENCOURAGEMENTS

I've taught on W3 in workshops literally hundreds of times—it's what I teach at Techstars on day one and has been adopted by the majority of managing directors across Techstars as well as many other accelerators. On day one, all the companies coming into the program are both feeling highly confident and highly insecure. They are feeling great and confident because they just became part of an elite 1 percent of companies who actually get accepted into Techstars, but insecure because by the time they're halfway into this workshop, they start to recognize just how much they do not know and how much work they still have to do to build a meaningful and repeatable business.

This chapter is absolutely essential to nail if you want to build the best, most profitable, and biggest business possible. *Do not rush through it.*

There will be parts that feel tedious, and there will be times when you have the urge to skip part of an exercise because it feels tedious or redundant or because you "just know." If you find yourself feeling that way, take a pause. Remember, we wrote this book to give you a simple-to-follow format to building a strong foundation. But simple doesn't always mean easy. With running a company, simple almost *never* means easy. This is hard work.

The mental image I like to give is like someone digging a ditch that is 100 feet × 100 feet × 100 feet deep. It's simple to see what needs to be done—just dig a hole, right? It's a simple task to understand. But if all you have is a shovel (or just your hands), that simple task will be difficult to complete.

Think of this chapter (and the entire book) in that way: the concepts are simple, but the work is hard.

Embrace the work, and let's *dig* in!

## HOW TO FIND YOUR W3

To demonstrate the deceptive power of W3, I'm going to walk you through how I introduce the concept during workshops. If you have the opportunity as you follow along, try the exercises yourself and see if you get the same aha moments.

I kick off the W3 workshop by asking the representatives for each company to take one minute (and only one minute) and write down their answers to these three questions:

1. Whom are you selling to?
2. What are they buying?
3. Why are they buying it?

When the time is up, I ask them if that time felt fast, just right, or like they had plenty of time. Everyone usually feels like one minute was more than enough time.

It should be simple, right? The answers to those three questions are why you exist as a company.

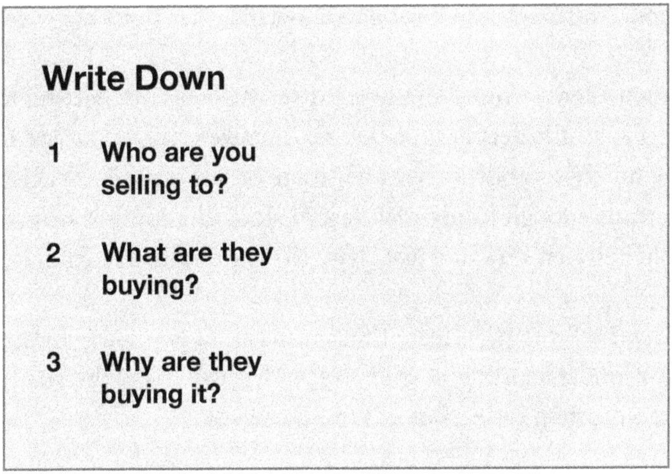

### Write Down

1 Who are you selling to?

2 What are they buying?

3 Why are they buying it?

Figure 1.1

Then I ask the companies to answer another question: *How do you know?* I ask them to both list the data and the opinions they have that lead them to believe each of their answers.

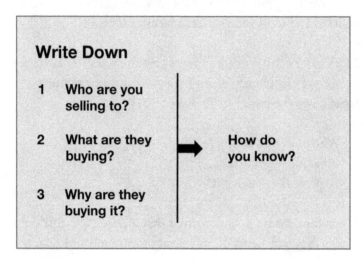

**Write Down**

1   Who are you
    selling to?

2   What are they          How do
    buying?                you know?

3   Why are they
    buying it?

Figure 1.2

This time, I give the companies ninety seconds, and I love watching what starts to happen next. I remind them to think about the data they have, the opinions they have, and to also think about the things they'd *want* to know that they don't know yet.

When I look around the room, I see their brains starting to engage a little deeper than before. And even still, at the end of the ninety seconds, everyone is more or less done. I ask again if it was enough time or felt fast or slow. The room is usually split between slow and just right. No one ever says it felt fast.

Next, I tell them, "Great. That means all of you likely have a clear understanding of your W3, which will make the rest of the workshop easier. But let's test ourselves."

The next part of the exercise is six minutes long, broken into four equal sections. The companies break into groups of two. For the first section, one founder will explain to a founder from a different company their W3 and how they know it. The second founder just listens and writes down what they are hearing and what questions they have. They can't talk during this time. During the next section, the listening founder repeats back what they heard and asks questions.

Afterward, they switch, and the second founder shares their W3, and the first founder just listens and writes notes. Again, when that time is up, they switch—now with the first founder asking the questions and the second founder responding.

**Break up into groups of 2 companies**

**Share your answers with each other**

**No verbal responses to questions**

**Write down what you noticed and what questions you have**

Figure 1.3

At the end of the six minutes, I call everyone back to center. This time, when I ask the question, "Did that feel fast, slow, or the right amount of time?" their answers are different. One hundred percent of the time, everyone felt like it was too fast. Neither party had enough time to talk about their company in a way that truly resonated with the other person.

Think about that for a second. Each founder literally had double the time to get their W3 articulated with time for Q&A, yet no one felt like they had enough time. Now extrapolate that to when you are talking to early investors or early customers.

If you aren't able to clearly articulate your W3, which is essentially your entire value proposition in three minutes, to someone whose attention you have in a controlled environment, what do you think your success will be in an environment where you have to grab someone's attention in much less time?

The next part of the exercise is one of my favorite parts. I ask everyone, "What happened there and how do you feel?"

The language from workshop to workshop will vary, but the themes that emerge are all the same:

1. "I thought I was clearly articulating my business, but I have a lot of work to do to make it clear."
2. "I realized that while I have strong conviction, I don't really have enough quantifiable or validated data to prove that I'm right."
3. "Holy shit, we still have a lot of work to do!"

These emotions are exactly what we're looking for.

Although strong conviction is essential to building your vision, until you have data, you shouldn't go too far in any one direction. The sooner you realize that, the better chance you will have of identifying your *real* W3 quickly—at least in its first iteration—so that you can get to scaling your business.

Think of it this way: Let's say you are in Kansas, where it's flat in every direction, and you have no phone or map with you. Then someone blindfolds you and spins you around, takes off the blindfold, and says, "Walk to Little Rock, Arkansas." What would you do?

You'd probably look around, look up and down, recall your geography class, maybe look at the sun to find north, south, east, and west, and then head off in a reasonable direction. The question is, would you just walk blindly until one day you hopefully found yourself in Little Rock? Or would you keep looking for signposts and collect additional data along the way to prove whether you are headed in the right direction?

Do you think you'd stop and ask people for directions along the way? If each person seemed credible and confident in their answers, as the hours and days went on, do you think you'd ask more and more people for directions to confirm you are headed in the right direction?

That is exactly what we are doing here. You know where you are as a business, and you know where you want to go. Now it's time to start making your way there. To do that, you must start with a W3 and what it will be one day at scale, then start navigating toward it. Your first W3 is a theory on your direction. Then you can begin collecting data and talking to lots and lots of people along the way to prove whether you are right or even why you may not be.

As you go through these questions, work with your founding team and executive team if you have one. It's not only critical that *you* understand all this and believe it deeply, but that the entire team and entire company needs to understand and believe it, too. When that happens—and when you can see you have enough data to believe you are right—that is when the magic happens.

## W1: WHO DO I BELIEVE IS MY CUSTOMER?

Your *who* is the reason you exist. Your *who* defines the entire potential for your business. At full scale, your *who* defines your total addressable market. And to one day reach your full potential, you need to take the first step. Remember, you may know for sure that you are headed to your "Arkansas," but right now, you only have a theory of which direction to go.

Defining your *who* should start to get uncomfortable for you. You will probably feel like you are (greatly) limiting your ability to grow or even reach your entire addressable market because you've made your *who* too narrow. As you go through this part of the exercise, keep in mind that this is not where you are ending. This is simply where you are starting so you can begin to get a very deep understanding of all the attributes of your ideal customer's profile.

For the purposes of defining our *who*, slowing down means developing the narrowest and most specific definition of whom you believe your customers are (or could be)—both today and in the near future. You want your definition of *who* to be so narrow and specific that even *you* think your business will be small if those are your only customers. You'll worry that investors won't see the full potential, and you'll even wonder if it's worth building the business if your customer base is so specific.

That's exactly how I want you to feel. That doesn't mean it's where we are going to end. It's just where we are starting so we have a tight control group to focus on to get the deepest understanding of our (initial) *who* as possible.

The ultimate proof is when your *who* is so narrow and specific that you know, with 100 percent confidence, that every single time you have a conversation, it will result in a sale (within an appropriate time frame for your business).

Yes, you read that correctly. In your first iteration of your *who*, your goal is to define your customer group so tightly that 100 percent of your conversations result in early sales. Even if your entire target list is 0.0001 percent of the entire market, you'll have absolute confidence that you will make a sale with every conversation.

Why? you ask. Good question. The answer is that once you know your *who* that perfectly and that intimately, you will be able to identify and define every single attribute of why that *who* makes a perfect customer. When you have that long list of attributes, it becomes exponentially easier to grow and expand your *who* by testing each attribute—adding, changing, and eliminating attributes along the way to all the peripheral *who* groups until you have ultimately expanded to the entire potential universe of *whos*.

When you take this approach, another magical thing happens. It directly informs your product roadmap (the plan for what you should be validating and what's ready to be built) and financial model in a very predictable way, and it makes the concepts in this entire book even more impactful.

You may still be scratching your head a little about what I mean by the most narrow and specific definition of *who*, so let me give you an example. We'll use Business.com, where I was Vice-President of Sales and Client Services and which I scaled to nearly $80M in revenue.

Founded in 1999 by serial entrepreneur and investor Jake Winebaum, Business.com was a search engine and directory for businesses. Small and medium businesses would go to Business.com to search for products and services they were looking for. We made money through the businesses that advertised on the site.

In theory, any business could advertise on Business.com, and likewise, any business could purchase the products and services that were being advertised. Based on that description, who is my *who*? Conventional wisdom would suggest that it was any business. But where would we start with something like that? How would we know when we had the right buyers and sellers? How would we know if we didn't have the right matches?

There is a very dangerous trap here that many businesses fall into. We've all seen them: they get some decent traction out of the gate, raise some good money to grow faster, get to a few million in revenue, and then flatline. Many never see their full potential and ultimately fail because their unit economics aren't strong enough to keep them alive and their focus isn't narrow enough to get to strong unit economics.

As a marketplace, Business.com had both a "seller" *who* (the business that paid us to advertise on Business.com) and a "buyer" *who* (the business that came to our site to find products and services from those advertisers). A different department was responsible for attracting each one. Our sales department was responsible for the seller *who*, and the product and marketing department was responsible for the buyer *who*. I'll focus here on the seller, the customer who actually paid us, but note that we went through this same exercise to figure out exactly which buyers we wanted to come to our site.

After countless tests, this is where we eventually settled for Business.com's *who*, the businesses that purchased ads on our site.

**Business.com's *who***: *Small and medium-sized businesses (SMBs) that had "shorter sale cycle" products and services, things that typically didn't need much research before someone made a purchase.*

From there, we narrowed down further. Those SMBs were also:

- In a product or service category on Business.com where we had a high level of page traffic and a sufficient number of existing sellers already on that page
- *Already buying* advertising on Google
- A top-ten advertiser on Google.

So now we understood the types of products and services our *who* sold and some key behaviors they were already doing. But we didn't stop there. We narrowed it down even further. Those SMBs also needed to:

- Have someone whose core responsibility was digital acquisition
- Measure results from their advertising campaigns on a regular basis so that they could see their own return on investment (ROI) from advertising on Business.com
- Incentivize the individual in the company purchasing the ads so that they earned more money if they improved their key metrics.

That was our *who*. When all those pieces fell into place, not only did we close the sale 100 percent of the time, but also our churn rate was less than 1 percent.

When we came to this level of specificity, we went from roughly $7M in annual revenue to $80M in about eighteen months (and then sold the company).

Now, did we sometimes sell outside of those tight criteria? Sure. But when we did, we tracked what attributes were different in those cases so we could learn and continue to expand peripherally. When we started seeing trends in those new attributes, we'd expand our focus.

Early on, those new cohorts would inevitably have lower close rates and higher churn, but because we knew what attributes were different, we were able to adapt. We would evolve the product, alter the messaging, or in some cases, even decide that this new customer set was not for us (at least right then).

### WHAT NOW?

Define your *who* as narrowly and specifically as possible. Write down all the (known) attributes you believe are in your *who* and go test them (along with your *what* and *why* when we get them) to see where you are right and wrong. When you believe you can achieve a 100 percent close rate with your known *who*, start to experiment with those attributes to broaden your potential customer set using the same methodology.

Before you move on, write all of that down. Take ten to twenty minutes and put on paper the most specific attributes of who you believe your *who* is today. Then feel free to keep reading.

## W2: WHAT DO I BELIEVE MY CUSTOMER IS BUYING FROM ME?

When I'm out delivering workshops on W3, at this point, I start to see this little light bulb go off for most people.

The conversation usually starts something like this. I tell them, "There is a difference between what you are selling and what your customer is buying. Can anyone explain what the difference is?"

Crickets.

It's the difference between what you do and what you do *for your customer.*

Let me call this out bluntly: We're all busy. Your customer doesn't give a shit what you do, but they *do* care what you do for *them*. It's that simple. You just need to put yourself in the frame of mind of your customer. Instead of leading with pride about the kickass product you've built, lead with how that product is going to impact their work.

Sometimes customers can make the connection between what you do and what you do for them for themselves, especially when your market is more mature. But why do you want to give them more work to do? Make it easy for them. Make it clear: what will you do for them?

In the words of marketing expert Theodore Levitt, "People don't want to buy a quarter-inch drill. They want a quarter-inch hole!"

Let me give you another example using Business.com. Put in the simplest form, we sold search. Our customers did not buy search, but search is the *what* we sold. They bought one of three things: sales, leads, or research.

Now let's put that in context. If I went to my customer and said, "Hey, buy search from me," they may or may not understand what that means to them. But if I understand that they are looking to buy *leads*, then I could go to them and say, "Hey, buy leads from me." Now there is no ambiguity to what they get—no time wasted on explanations to connect dots for them—and we can get deeper into a buying conversation as their partner rather than pitching like just another salesperson.

For Business.com, we had a very tactical *what*, but yours doesn't have to be.

Sometimes that *what* is something squishier such as time or peace of mind, and sometimes it's more than one thing. Regardless of your *what*, it's important to figure it out as early as possible. Aside from helping you with your pitch, it also directly impacts your revenue formula (coming in Chapter 2) and your product roadmap (Chapter 3).

To demonstrate that last point, I'm going to use my experience at the company BlackLocus, where I was VP of Sales.

BlackLocus was a data analytics company for the retail industry. When I joined, the team believed that the *what* that our customers bought was:

"data on companies' competitors."

Of course (as you now know), this wasn't what our customers bought. This was what we sold. After working with the team to understand what they actually thought we sold, they distilled the *what* to:

> "Telling our customers who their competitors were, based on products they sold in common."

Now we had something that was reframed from the perspective of our customer. But the problem with this version was that it was just incorrect.

The difference ended up being extremely subtle but vital to our actual customers. Our customers already knew who their competitors were, generally speaking. What they didn't know was who their biggest competitors were *at the product level.* Not every one of our customers' competitors sold the same products that they did. We gave our customers the ability to know who sold the same products they did and at what price so they could know who their competitors *really* were for their most important products. That was our real *what.*

BlackLocus's *what*: Competitive insight into the most important products, which competitors sell your most important products and at what price they sell them.

When we figured that difference out, it not only helped us refine our *who*, but it also informed our product roadmap once we understood what mattered—and it made it much easier to understand their *why* (the third W).

That simple, nuanced switch in what you do *for them* rather than what you do helps you quickly put everyone on the same page in terms of whether you and a potential customer can work together. It can usually help you more quickly figure out whether your *who* is right because you now have data that suggests your *who* actually cares about your *what!*

**WHAT NOW?**

Think about your *what* in the context of what you do for your customer (not just what you do)—even if the difference seems subtle. Spend time talking to prospects and customers, really trying to understand *what* they are actually buying from you.

Take five to ten minutes to write down a few theories on what you believe your customer is going to (or already is) buy(ing) from you. Then move on to *why*.

## W3: WHY DOES MY CUSTOMER BUY FROM ME?

The *why* is often the most overlooked of the W3 because most founders swing too far in one of two directions: either they think it's obvious and implied, or they just don't think about it at all. But sometimes we get it wrong, so it's important to *really* know.

The *why* shows you the value your customers get from your product. It shows you what matters to them. Here's an example using Business.com.

From the work we had done testing with customers, we knew that the businesses that advertised on Business.com were coming to buy leads from us. That was our *what*. We didn't sell advertising; we sold leads. But why did leads matter to our customers? Because they want to nurture those leads into sales to increase their revenue.

Now we understood what mattered to our customers—nurturing leads into sales and increasing revenue. More importantly, we could also understand how *our customer* measured that *why*. At Business.com, it was simple: they measured it by seeing whether the leads they bought increased sales and revenue. When a customer can tell you the value they receive from your product and they can show you how they are measuring that value, you have the ultimate data you can collect to prove your W3.

Please reread that. It's not about how *you* measure the customer's *why*—it's about how they measure it. Because if they can't measure that *why*, then it becomes exponentially harder to justify the exchange of money for *what* you're selling. When they can and do measure the *why*, it becomes exponentially easier to identify when and how well your product fits their needs, which will result in a sale.

The best way to get that understanding is to simply ask them. Ask your customers, "What is the value you get from my product or service?" and then follow up with, "How do you know? How do you measure it?"

## WHEN YOU SELL TO BUSINESSES, YOU ACTUALLY HAVE TWO *WHYS*

For companies that sell to organizations and not just individuals, there are really two *whys*: why the business (as a whole) buys your product or service, and why the actual buyer buys it.

In those situations, the actual buyer *why* is really critical, especially in the early days in helping define your *who*. Let me give you an example from Business.com. When we finally figured out our W3, I could say something like, "I sell to SMBs who buy leads because those leads result in increased sales for their business."

Now let's take that scenario and say that our individual buyer was great at their job. They already bought search at Google and other sites. Let's also say that they were already on track to hit or exceed their goals, so buying leads from Business.com would not get them any extra bonuses, raises, or promotions, and it would result in a little extra work to track an additional lead source. In that case, there is no motivation for them to work with Business.com. In fact, there is motivation to *not* work with us.

So what do we do? First of all, this tells me our *who* is off here, even if by a little. Either the person who I think is my buyer in this particular company is wrong (and I need to go to a different person in the company), or the company type was wrong and this company isn't really part of my *who* yet).

Remember, the goal with the first cut of your W3 is to identify the profile that gets you a sale 100 percent of the time. In this case, only one attribute is different in that the actual buyer doesn't have the correct incentives in place to buy. You can either move on to a buyer who does or spin your wheels trying to convince someone to do something for you that doesn't necessarily benefit them. You could also choose to go around them, which would take them out of your current *who* and would create a different buyer profile as well. At Business.com, we chose to pass on those types of buyers initially because we knew we'd spin our wheels and likely get nowhere. We'd keep checking in until their incentives changed, at which time, they did fall in our W3 and bought every time.

## WHAT NOW?

Every customer has a *why* for buying your product. When selling to businesses, you have two *whys*: *why* it matters to the business and *why* it matters to the individual buyer. In order to truly understand these, you need to understand how your customer will measure success. That measurement and the data on impact will inform your longer-term *why*.

Write down your theory on the *why* question, how you believe your customers will measure them, and how you can ensure they have the right tools to measure it. Then make the *why* an active and collaborative part of your conversation with all your prospects and customers.

If you've made it to this point, then you have written down a clear theory of your W3. Congratulations on this important first step. Even if your business is a little more mature and you've been selling for a while, you should now have a clearer and better-articulated version of what you've been doing to this point.

There are (at least) two things to do from here. The first is to keep holding the mindset that you are in data collection mode and trying to prove (and disprove) your W3—and all along, playing with the attributes, as you gain confidence, to continue growing your total addressable market.

The second is to keep reading. If you are on a roll, keep reading (and working), but be forewarned that the next chapter comes with at least an equal amount of work. So if you need to step away for an hour (or a couple of days), that's fine. The work you have done in this chapter (and will continue to do through your customer conversations) is critical to getting the most out of the rest of this book. Keep doing the work to build an amazing foundation!

## CHAPTER 2

# REVENUE FORMULA

## (BY AMOS SCHWARTZFARB)

*How do I create value and ultimately revenue?*

Trevor and I sat next to Haley and Steve Bohon, CEO and COO of SkillPop, staring at a blank whiteboard. SkillPop offers live, expert-led classes and workshops. They had seen impressive growth with their in-person classes in and around Charlotte, North Carolina, and now they needed to figure out how to take that growth to new places. We asked ourselves: *What are the key variables of SkillPop's growth?* Steve started scribbling potential variables on the board: the number of cities SkillPop had classes in, the number of classes in each of those cities, the number of students that attended each class, the price they charged for each class. We started to feel like we were getting somewhere.

On the surface, it looked like a sensible model. If you increased any one of those things—cities, classes, students per class, price—revenue would go up. But something didn't feel right. Haley had been inside this business for years and knew intuitively that the real driver of growth was something that wasn't on the board yet. She knew it. She just hadn't figured out how to articulate it in a way she could begin to rigorously test and repeat.

Suddenly, it came to her: not students, *teachers*.

People came to SkillPop not just because they liked the classes but because they loved the teachers. What if they stopped thinking about teachers as just the provider of the service but actually as a primary driver of growth in the business?

We wiped the board clean and started to write a new revenue formula, this time based around SkillPop's teachers. It was a major breakthrough, and now three years later, the company has continued to grow (even through the COVID pandemic) and has become more profitable from a unit economics perspective all along the way.

## YOU CAN'T BE METRICS-DRIVEN IF YOU DON'T HAVE A REVENUE FORMULA

When I ran my first Techstars Austin program in January of 2016, I had the perfect plan. On day one, I delivered a workshop on key performance indicators (KPIs).

It made complete sense as I was planning it. I was deeply committed to helping this first group quickly become metrics-driven businesses. I also wanted to give a KPI workshop because I know how hard it can be to actually figure out the right metrics for your business and ultimately become metrics driven.

I had prepared for a few weeks so that I could deliver a great talk on what KPIs were, all the different types that exist, and the ways they can be used. I felt like I had created an amazing class to teach people all about the theory of KPIs, and I fully believed that with this foundation, those founders would be able to identify their KPIs more quickly and start growing fast.

Well, the lecture fell flat.

Actually, flat is an understatement. It straight-up sucked. I left people scratching their heads, having more questions than answers, and having no framework to figure out what *their* KPIs should be. I was mortified, and more importantly, I felt like I had already failed the first ten companies coming through Techstars Austin after just one workshop.

I went home that night feeling like shit and wondered how I could quickly come up with something to salvage the lecture and give the companies something meaty they could work on to become metrics driven.

Then it struck me: I had to turn my KPI lecture into a revenue formula workshop!

The term *revenue formula* is new to most people; if you have heard it, you likely think about it as a sales formula. It's not. Before I can expand on the definition, let me give you a little context on how I got there in the first place.

By the time I became the managing director at Techstars Austin, I had seen and been part of three metrics-driven businesses (Hot-Jobs, Business.com, and BlackLocus), and I had seen just how big and quick the impact could be once the business (a) figured out what their true core metrics were and (b) got the entire company rallied around those metrics (as well as all the underlying metrics).

I had also been involved in a fourth company, Joust, where we would say we were metrics driven, but really, we had no idea what truly drove our business. That business failed—to no surprise.

The place where I witnessed this impact the most was at Business.com.

In Chapter 1, I talk a lot about how identifying our W3 was a pivotal time for the company in figuring out how to grow and scale. After that, we saw phenomenal results in a very short amount of time that resulted in a sale to R. H. Donnelly for $350M.

Well, W3 wasn't the only element that enabled that growth. We also had an amazing executive team, a world-class board, a phenomenal CEO and leader, and the ability to recruit. Timing played a big role in our success as well.

There was one other thing that tied that all together: figuring out our revenue formula.

We knew exactly which were the four most important, top-line KPIs in our business, and even more importantly, we built systems to figure out what drove those top-line metrics, the metrics that drove those, and so on. We had the absolute deepest understanding, from a math and metrics perspective, that I had ever seen in a business. It was completely transformative.

In a second, I'll share exactly what our revenue formula was for Business.com. For now, let me define what a revenue formula is.

## WHAT IS A REVENUE FORMULA?

A revenue formula is the mathematical equation of your business. It's how you turn your product, sales, marketing, technology, customer service, and every other department into math that makes sense as you run and grow your business.

Another way to express the revenue formula is to call it your business model. Even though that's technically correct, I don't like to start there. I believe the definition of business model has been somewhat muddied to become more high level, such as the "marketplace business model" or the "SaaS business model." Because those types of examples have become common language, it creates an unnatural pause. In a common marketplace where businesses like Business.com or Uber or Candidly exist, the actual core elements of each of their revenue formulas are not identical (even if the structures are very similar).

Identifying your revenue formula is absolutely critical to building and growing your business because it gives you maximum control of the drivers that matter in your business. I may be stating the obvious here, but I'm going to do it anyway so there is no confusion. Without a revenue formula, you cannot build a repeatable business.

When you figure out your revenue formula, you will have the ability to truly understand, measure, prioritize, focus, and leverage the most important parts of your business. It becomes the common language at every level in your organization. It gives each member of each team a clean and clear direction on what they should be working on *and* why it matters to their job and the business.

Equally important, it becomes a framework to ignore everything else (yes, even those bright and shiny new ideas).

I'll go so far as to say that even if you are already very metrics driven but don't truly know your revenue formula, you're likely to fail—or at least never achieve your optimal potential as a business. The revenue formula allows you to put your metrics into context—to understand the real levers in your business and what matters most for generating growth.

When you figure out your revenue formula, that is when the true magic happens.

## THE ORIGINS OF THE REVENUE FORMULA

There are plenty of successful companies out there who do know their revenue formula but don't use that terminology. Likewise, the framework we will go into later in this chapter is only one way to find yours. I also want to be clear that I did not invent this concept. I learned it, primarily at Business. com, and you will see versions of it in the growth stories of many of today's biggest tech companies. But I did turn it into a framework that any company can use.

The power of the revenue formula is that even at the earliest stages of your business, it will help you figure out what you should (and shouldn't) be working on and, if you even have a valid business at all, by using math rather than emotion as your guiding light.

Let me say that again: use math rather than emotion. At the end of the day, no matter what your business is (business-to-business [B2B], consumer product goods, consumer app, etc.), it's nothing more than a complex math equation. All of the story and theater that we layer on top of the math that motivate us, our customers, and our communities are important, but never lose sight of the fact that business (and life) is three parts math and one part theater.[2]

## *YOUR* REVENUE FORMULA

We've defined a revenue formula as the mathematical equation of your business. If you are an early-stage company, no matter how strong your conviction, all you have at best is a *hypothesis* of what your revenue formula will be one day when you are ready to move from repeatability to the scale phase. Until then, it is your job to prove (and disprove) why your revenue formula is right.

Trying to prove it right is important, but it can also be a slippery slope. As optimistic founders, we want to believe we are right. This means it's very easy for confirmation bias to slip in and convince us that the trends we see in the math will persist over time. That is why, at each stage when you think you are headed in the right direction, you also need to shift your thinking to "Why might I *not* be correct?" As scary and undesirable as that sounds, it's imperative for you to go down that path just as often as you attempt to prove you're right.

And guess what? Sometimes the answers suck. You find out that you don't really have a business, or at least a big enough business. But when you get it right, you have collected enough data so that you and your team (and your investors, if you have any) have the data-driven confidence to pile money into your business and accelerate growth at rocket ship pace.

---

2    One day, I'll write a book about this, too.

## GROWING FAST WITH NO REVENUE FORMULA

We've all heard about companies that raise huge rounds, grow huge teams, have top-line revenue growth that looks like they are headed toward unicorn status, and then suddenly, they start to fizzle or crash and burn.

As outsiders, we can point to any number of (theoretical) reasons why this happens, such as poor management, new competition, market conditions. Although those can all be factors, the biggest one is that they really never figured out their revenue formula, scaled way too early, and were ultimately *way* more fragile than one would think. All those things are contributors, but the core of all of them is that they didn't have a strong handle on their revenue formula. If they had, in most cases the math would have navigated them away from failure.

## THE REVENUE FORMULA QUEST

Figuring out your revenue formula is nothing short of a quest. Not a simple exercise, not an adventure, but a long journey. You're going to have to do a lot of hard work. You'll hit tons of obstacles that you'll need to navigate through or around, and you'll need to be prepared to be wrong a lot more than you are right.

I think of *The Lord of the Rings* here. You're going to have to travel through forests and over mountains and through muddy bogs. You'll encounter dragons and evil creatures along the way, all trying to knock you off course. Just when you think you've reached the end, you'll realize, "Oh shit, this is only the halfway point!"

Buckle up and get ready for a long ride. If you are fortunate, you have a great team all working together and in the same direction.

Of course, if you don't think you have it in you, stop now, close the book, and go get a job at a big company.

Yeah, I knew you'd keep reading.

The steps of the quest are simple, but that doesn't mean they're easy. You'll write down your current theory of your revenue formula. As you do, envision me sitting next to you asking you (over and over) one question: "Why do you believe that to be true?" Once you feel like you are at a decent starting point, we'll then look one level deeper and identify all of the drivers of each value in your formula. Then we'll take it yet *another* level deeper and identify all the subdrivers of those drivers.

First, let's start with a few examples of revenue formulas. I'll talk you through some of the details before I put you to work. The first example is from Business.com, which I introduced in Chapter 1. The second example is from Chowbotics, a company that sells robots that make food. Their customers are hospitals, schools, and public cafeterias.

## THE BUSINESS.COM REVENUE FORMULA

Recall that Business.com was a search engine and directory that enabled SMBs to sell their products and services to other SMBs. We were very much a B2B company, and the core product we sold was search (just like the search you buy on Google today). The difference was that we only had business products and services. At the highest level, we made money when someone clicked on a search result on the Business.com website that one of our customers had paid us for (an ad). Similar to Google, we'd charge a Cost per Click (CPC). If we charged our customer $1.00 CPC, then we made $1.00 (gross) every time someone clicked on an ad.

**Business.com revenue formula:**

$$\text{Visits} \times \text{Coverage} \times \text{Conversion Rate} \times \text{CPC} = \text{Revenue}$$

Here are our definitions of each:

- **Visits:** The number of people who showed up on any page of Business.com regardless of if/what content we had on that page.
- **Coverage:** Our nomenclature for the percentage of pages, where people were going, that we had at least one piece of clickable content on.
- **Conversion:** The percentage of people who actually clicked on a piece of content (whether or not we made money from it).
- **CPC:** The cost per click that our advertisers would pay *us* for each one of our visitors who clicked on an ad (i.e., paid piece of content).
- **Revenue:** Gross revenue generated to Business.com.

**Visits x Coverage x Conversion Rate x Cost Per Click = Revenue**

**Visits =** number of people who went to *business.com*

**Coverage =** % of pages on *business.com* that had content for visitor to interact with

**Conversion Rate =** % of people who clicked on content from *business.com* page

**CPC =** the rate *business.com* charges our advertisers for each click on their content

Figure 2.1

Now, let's say 1,000 people came to Business.com over the period of a month and 80 percent of the pages they landed on had some piece of clickable content. Let's also say that 80 percent of the people who landed on a page with clickable content actually clicked on a piece of content. And finally, let's assume that the average CPC across those pages was $1.86. In that scenario, Business.com would generate $1,190.40 in gross revenue:

> 1,000 visits × 80 percent of pages with clickable content × 80 percent of people who clicked on that content × $1.86 cost per click = $1,190.40 monthly revenue.

You might think that this exercise is only valuable to your sales team, but there's more behind each value in the formula. In fact, when you start to unpack the things that drive each of these values, you'll see that they touch every part of the business.

- **Visits:** Although visits were primarily driven by our market-ing department, in order to understand what type of visitor we should be driving to what page to optimize revenue, it required our product team and technology team to work closely together to make sure that *when* someone landed on a page, the content on that page was the right content, delivered in the right format so that a user would click on something truly relevant to them. The sales team had nothing to do with this.

- **Coverage:** This metric was driven by a combination of our sales team, product team, and technology team. It was driven by sales because we needed to know which pages had the largest opportunity to generate revenue—a combination of where we had the most traffic, with the least (existing) content, at the optimal max price per click.[3] That combination of variables gave the sales team a stack rank of revenue opportunity by page, which sales and marketing then cross-referenced to a list of all potential advertisers to those pages. That gave sales their lead lists, in real time, based on real opportunity.

- **Conversion:** I love this one because it truly touched almost every department. It obviously touched on product because we had to deliver the best experience to the end user who wanted to actually click on something. It touched on technology to build the vision our product team had around an optimal product. It touched on marketing because we had to make sure that the right people were showing up on a page (which required their data) and the right messaging was in place for those people. And it required sales to not only sell advertisers but the *right* advertisers so that the products and services being offered were the right ones.

- **CPC:** The obvious owner of this metric was sales because we were the ones selling the advertiser at the highest dollar value possible (but not so high that the conversion cost didn't make sense for them). It also required our technology

---

3    At some point on every page, we'd hit a max price and diminishing returns for adding additional advertisers.

team to build and maintain a system so that our customers had both real-time visibility into their conversion metrics as well as price-adjusting algorithms to ensure we optimized the order of the advertiser—not only by price but also by click-through rate (CTR).

As you can see, even though the revenue formula clearly shows how you make money, it's only partially about sales or the sales team at all. Instead, it's a full, mathematical view into how each of the departments contribute to growing revenue.

There is also one metric that is not overtly expressed here but that is of the utmost importance: churn. Although we didn't include it explicitly in our revenue formula, we used the same thinking to clearly identify the drivers that affected churn.

One of the things I prided myself on at Business.com was that we had extremely low churn. Keep in mind that between W3 and our revenue formula, we had a strong, data-driven understanding of who our customers were and how we made money.

Because of W3, marketing knew exactly whom they should be targeting. And because of a combination of W3 and the direction provided by coverage, conversion, and CPC, sales also knew exactly the profile of whom we should target. This combination meant that the users we were directing to our customers' ads were the right customers to convert and generate business for them. Because we tracked conversion data and CPC data, we knew the optimal price for our customers that we could still make money from and the right kind of customers for them. This combination made it easy (for us) to match the right visitor with the right advertiser so that everyone had a delightful experience. This translated into visitors coming back to Business.com using us as their main resource for finding and buying the products and services they needed, *and* it meant that our customers generated enough revenue with enough margin to continue being customers. In fact, they were growing along with us.

There is one final piece to controlling churn here, which is outside of the revenue formula—that is, salesperson compensation. I cover this in depth in *Sell More Faster*, but the gist is that the comp plan should incentivize closing not only high-paying but long-term customers in the specific categories or pages that generated the most revenue.

## THE CHOWBOTICS REVENUE FORMULA

This example may seem less complicated on the surface, but as you will see, there are many drivers and subdrivers that make this a complex equation as well. Chowbotics are robots that make food, specifically salads, and are typically found in places such as airports, hospitals, or small cafeterias that don't have salad bars. Chowbotics sells their robots to their customers, and then the customers decide if they will charge for salads or not.

Chowbotics's revenue formula is a SaaS (salad as a service) model. More specifically:

Number of Units × Cost/Unit/Month × Months Installed = Revenue

Here is a definition for each value:

- **Number of Units:** The number of salad robots deployed (for a customer and/or in the world).

- **Cost/Unit/Month:** This is how much Chowbotics charges, each month, for their salad robot to be deployed at a customer location.
- **Months Installed:** This is the number of months that a customer has a salad robot deployed at their location.

**Units x Cost/Month x Months Installed = Revenue**

**# of Units** = number of salad robots deployed (at a customer or in the world)

**Cost/Month** = monthly charge to customer for robot deployed at customer

**Months Installed** = number of months a cusomter has robot deployed at their location

Figure 2.2

Let's say for simplicity's sake that Chowbotics had one hundred customers who each had three units. That would be three hundred units deployed.

Now let's say the cost of each unit is $1,000 per month, and on average, a customer had their salad robots for thirty months. In this case, Chowbotics would make $9,000,000 in revenue:

300 units × $1,000 per unit × 30 months installed = $9,000,000 revenue

As with the Business.com example, we can then break down what is behind each value:

- **Number of Units:** On the surface, this is an easy, "How many robots are deployed, and what is the sales process?" But also, *how* do you know whom to target? What type of robot do you build? How do you figure out building the robots? There are also considerations around supplies, logistics, shipping, delivery, and so on. Many elements go into being able to deliver even a single robot, much less hundreds or thousands. This touches almost every department in the organization.

- **Cost/Unit/Month:** Although on the surface it might seem that most of this value is driven by sales, finance, engineering, and even marketing have a hand here. Not only do we need to figure out price elasticity, but we also need to make sure margins work. There should be an appropriate structure around payment and delivery to make sure both our balance sheet and our statement of cash flow work well together so we can stay in business.

- **Months Installed:** Again, on the surface it might seem like this is all driven by sales, but it's not. Product and engineering need to deliver both a machine that meets expectations as well as back-end analytics to the customer. The client service team needs to be driving customer satisfaction and improvements so that the thirty months turn into forty rather thirty.

## IDENTIFYING YOUR REVENUE FORMULA

How do you figure out your revenue formula? First, let me give you a sneak peek into what you will end up with.

| Visits | x | Coverage | x | Conversion Rate | x | CPC |
|---|---|---|---|---|---|---|

| **Direct** | **Sales** | **Coverage** | **Category** |
|---|---|---|---|
| Email | Inside | Sales | Top |
| Blog | Outside | Technology | Optimized |
| SEO | Reseller | Product | Type |
| Twitter | Account Mgmt | Marketing | Industry |
| LinkedIn | Affiliate | Google | Marketing |

| **Paid** | **Product** | **UX** | **Sales** |
|---|---|---|---|
| Google | Algo | Expert | Vertical |
| Facebook | Rev Optimize | Layout | Lead Gen |
| Twitter | Google Sub | Metrics | Team |
| LinkedIn | Website | My Testing | Industry |
| Ad Network | Build | Technology | Category |

| **Tradeshow** | **Technology** | **Testing** | **Google** |
|---|---|---|---|
| Booth | Algo | Analyst | Algo |
| Giveaway | Infrastructure | Platform | Optimization |
| Meeting | Servers | Unknown | Tech |
| Pre-Promo | Security | Reporting | API |
| Remarked | Build | Technology | Category |

| **PR** | **Google** | **Tech** | **Demand** |
|---|---|---|---|
| Tour | Algo | Algo | Coverage |
| Recurring | Metrics | Platform | Category |
| Local | API | Data | Lead Gen |
| National | Rep | Reporting | Depth |
| Trades | Unknown | Stability | Category |

| **Radio** | **Marketing** | **Layout** | **Saturation** |
|---|---|---|---|
| Local | Sales | Size | Depth |
| Time of Day | PR | Spacing | Coverage |
| Produce | Content | Depth | Demand |
| National | Support | Coverage | Lead Gen |
| Measure | Tradeshow | Color | Category |

Figure 2.3

What you see in the image is not just the Business.com revenue formula, but all the drivers and subdrivers for each value. At the end of this exercise, you will have a similar chart for your business, which will give you all the things you need to do in order to prove whether you are correct about your revenue formula.

## STEP 1: ESTABLISH A THEORY

| Visits | x | Coverage | x | Conversion Rate | x | CPC |
|---|---|---|---|---|---|---|
| | | | | | | |
| | | | | | | |
| | | | | | | |
| | | | | | | |
| | | | | | | |

Figure 2.4

Let's start by putting a stake in the ground. Get out a piece of paper or sit down at your computer. Using the examples above, write down your current theory of your revenue formula. In fact, don't read past this paragraph until you do. Without overthinking and trying to be perfect, take your time. If you can rattle it off in thirty seconds, that's fine, but if it takes more time, that is okay, too. Come up with something that articulates what you think it is today so that we can go out and prove it right or wrong.

Remember, this is a long quest. It took Business.com eight years to figure it out. Today, you are just taking the very first steps. The important thing is to have a starting point. Expect that you are probably wrong because if you weren't, you'd already have rocket ship growth.

Here are some common questions (and my responses) that I usually get right about now:

**"We have more than one product; should we make a revenue formula for each?"**

If you are an early-stage company, you can't have two products, whether you like it or not. You need to decide right now what business you want to build and focus on that. You can always come back to the other later when either you've hit repeatability or at least validity with the first. But as an early-stage company, you cannot sell two products. You just do not have the time or resources. Even for more mature companies, it's better to focus on hitting repeatability for one product and then only moving to the next once you've achieved that.

**"We have more than one revenue stream; should we make a revenue formula for each?"**

No, you don't. In fact, you have *no* revenue streams—you've merely generated some revenue. A revenue stream means you are at repeatability. Pick the *one* you think will be your primary and go test it to see if you are right or wrong. Stop focusing on the other one.

I get a lot of pushback on those two responses, and although I realize sometimes the answers are not that binary, my challenge to you is to *make* it that binary. Simplify the thing you are really doing here, which is not yet growing your business, but validating whether your idea can even *be* a business.

There is plenty of time to add products and revenue streams once you've hit some level of repeatability or scale. Adding the complexity of products or revenue streams now just means you don't likely have enough conviction yet in one or the other to put all your focus there. If you don't have the conviction, then you shouldn't expect your team or potential investors to have that conviction either.

### "Is a revenue formula really just a sales funnel?"

It is a funnel—it is *not* a sales funnel or marketing funnel. It's a business funnel, a map of how everything moves in your business. Your business is just a series of funnels, and the revenue formula ties those funnels together.

### "I have a marketplace business; what should I do?"

Yes, marketplace businesses can be more complex. There are two great marketplace worksheets that I encourage all marketplace businesses to fill out. The first is by Bill Gurley, and the second is by Arteen Arabshahi.[4] For most marketplaces, one side of the market (usually supply) is easier to identify and put a stake in the ground on. The caution here is that you may be wrong, so you need to stay open-minded. And although you will have only

---

4    Bill Gurley: https://abovethecrowd.com/2012/11/13/all-markets-are-not-created-equal-10-factors-to-consider-when-evaluating-digital-marketplaces/. Arteen Arabshahi: https://arteenin.la/the-marketplace-calculator-229e5fb8b4d3.

one revenue formula, it's a complex formula that will require quite a bit more testing and work after your first assumption.

## STEP 2: IDENTIFY THE DRIVERS FOR YOUR KEY VALUES

| Visits | x | Coverage | x | Conversion Rate | x | CPC |
|---|---|---|---|---|---|---|
| Direct | | Sales | | Coverage | | Category |
| Paid | | Product | | UX | | Sales |
| Tradeshow | | Technology | | Testing | | Google |
| PR | | Google | | Tech | | Demand |
| Radio | | Marketing | | Layout | | Saturation |

Figure 2.5

The frame of mind here is simple: What are all the (known) things that can contribute to growing your top-line value? Think of this as the first-level list of either tasks you need to accomplish or substantiate to prove that the value you think should be in your formula *actually* should be.

For the sake of this book, we are going to take only one value from the Business.com example and outline all the things that drive it. However, your job is to go through this work for every value in your revenue formula. Additionally, we will come up with five drivers for our example value. When you do this exercise on your own, note that you may have less but likely more than five drivers per value.

Let's start by looking at our current revenue formula and pick a single value to work on. Have you picked your value? Once you have, start making a list of the next-level drivers that you need to either do or prove in order to move that value, which you should now think of as key metrics for your business.

Need a little help? We'll choose the visits value within the Business.com revenue formula to work on:

**Visits** × Coverage × Conversion × CPC = Revenue

Here are the five drivers I've come up with for visits, remembering that this is a list of things we do or prove in order to confirm that *visits* are actually a main part of our revenue formula:

1. **Direct:** People who came directly to the Business.com website.
2. **Paid:** People who came to the Business.com website because of a specific, paid, online acquisition tactic.
3. **Trade Shows:** People who came to Business.com because of a trade show that we either exhibited at or attended.
4. **PR:** People who came to Business.com because of our PR strategy and efforts.
5. **Radio:** People who came to Business.com because of a radio ad they heard.

As you are likely thinking, these are all obvious, and that is a good thing. It means we have a starting place and can start to develop a plan. More than likely, it also sparked two additional thoughts for you. The first is that there are so many more tactics we could employ to drive visits to Business.com, and you are correct. Remember, I'm keeping the list to five for the ease of following in this book, but your list will likely be much longer. It's also okay if it's not; just list the things that you currently think you need to do or prove in order to know, beyond a reasonable doubt, that your value is correct.

Hint: Your "gut" or intuition isn't good enough. You need to go get data. And you will almost certainly be adding to this list over time.

The other things this list is likely doing is making you wonder why are *these* the tactics and what proof do I have that these will work?

My answer is simple: I cannot know that for you. Our goal here is not to have all the answers but to figure out as many of the questions as possible so that we know what data we need to go get in order to prove our revenue formula is right (or not). With that in mind, as you create your list of drivers, have a side piece of paper where you are writing down all the questions, knowns, and unknowns. You'll use these lists both in this chapter and in the next chapter to validate assumptions and prioritization.

## STEP 3: IDENTIFY THE SUBDRIVERS FOR EACH DRIVER

Before we get into this next part, make sure you have some time, at minimum thirty minutes but ideally at least an hour, where you won't be interrupted. Turn off your email and silence your phone. This is tedious but mandatory if you want to make the most out of the rest of this book.

Although this section is going to sound a lot like the last one, it'll be roughly five times the work. Again, we will demonstrate only one driver to work on here, but you'll need to do this for every driver you've identified so far.

Let's start with our Business.com revenue formula:

Visits × Coverage × Conversion × CPC = Revenue

In step 2, we decided to work on visits, which gave us these five drivers: direct, paid, trade shows, PR, and radio.

We will use the paid driver here, which represented digital acquisition. The next step is to pick five subdrivers of paid. These are the more specific tactics that we need to actually do to see if paid is a valid tactic to drive the right users to Business.com. Here are the five subdrivers we've come up with and why:

1. **Google**—great for general search.
2. **Facebook (FB)**—Most business owners are always thinking about their business, even when on a nonbusiness social network.
3. **LinkedIn**—Business owners network here.
4. **Twitter**—Businesses and business owners congregate here for news and information.
5. **Vertical Ad Networks**—More specific to where business owners may spend some online time when working.

Keep in mind, right now this list is simply nothing more than a theory of where we might find our users and increase visits. If you've done your work on W3 (Chapter 1), then when you find the right channels, it'll be like shooting fish in a barrel. Without doing that work, it's more like shooting fish in the clouds—it's not really possible.

If you are thinking to yourself, "Shit, this is a lot of tedious work," recall my warning at the beginning of the chapter. If you are wondering if you really need to do this work, the answer is no. You do not *need* to do all this work. You can choose to skip it, but if you do, you will open the door for much more risk in execution. If you can't do a few tedious tasks now, consider whether you really have what it takes to build a long-term and meaningful business.

Anyway, if you don't list your subdrivers now, the next chapter will literally be useless. So get to work!

When you're finished, congratulate yourself. Whenever I teach this as a workshop, we stop here at the subdrivers. By this point, you get the gist of what needs to be done, and this often is where you can stop. But I'd like to challenge you to take it a step further.

Before you move on with this book, take a good look at all your subdrivers and ask yourself whether any of them have sub-subdrivers. Not all of them will, but some might.

Take fifteen more minutes and go through each of your subdrivers to see where you can go one level deeper. I personally haven't come across any *sub*-sub-subdrivers, but I'm sure there are some out there.

You don't need to go that deep for the purposes of this exercise, but keep it in mind. When you start going through the work of *actually figuring out what work you need to do*, just know that some of these tasks may need to get more granular.

When you are "done," your work should look something like the Business.com map of drivers. But there are a couple of things I want to point out. The first is that there will likely be tasks or tactics that overlap on that list. That's a good thing because it'll help you ultimately prioritize the work as well as clearly understand dependencies. The second is that not all the work will be (easily) measurable. That's okay, too. Solving the challenge of how to measure will have an added benefit of helping you build muscle around being truly metrics driven.

| Visits | x | Coverage | x | Conversion Rate | x | CPC |
|---|---|---|---|---|---|---|

| **Direct** | **Sales** | **Coverage** | **Category** |
|---|---|---|---|
| Email | Inside | Sales | Top |
| Blog | Outside | Technology | Optimized |
| SEO | Reseller | Product | Type |
| Twitter | Account Mgmt | Marketing | Industry |
| LinkedIn | Affiliate | Google | Marketing |
| **Paid** | **Product** | **UX** | **Sales** |
| Google | Algo | Expert | Vertical |
| Facebook | Rev Optimize | Layout | Lead Gen |
| Twitter | Google Sub | Metrics | Team |
| LinkedIn | Website | My Testing | Industry |
| Ad Network | Build | Technology | Category |
| **Tradeshow** | **Technology** | **Testing** | **Google** |
| Booth | Algo | Analyst | Algo |
| Giveaway | Infrastructure | Platform | Optimization |
| Meeting | Servers | Unknown | Tech |
| Pre-Promo | Security | Reporting | API |
| Remarked | Build | Technology | Category |
| **PR** | **Google** | **Tech** | **Demand** |
| Tour | Algo | Algo | Coverage |
| Recurring | Metrics | Platform | Category |
| Local | API | Data | Lead Gen |
| National | Rep | Reporting | Depth |
| Trades | Unknown | Stability | Category |
| **Radio** | **Marketing** | **Layout** | **Saturation** |
| Local | Sales | Size | Depth |
| Time of Day | PR | Spacing | Coverage |
| Produce | Content | Depth | Demand |
| National | Support | Coverage | Lead Gen |
| Measure | Tradeshow | Color | Category |

Figure 2.6

It's hard to overemphasize how powerful this document was for us at Business.com and how powerful it can be in your business. This was literally the map we used to drive revenue by ten times.

So where do you go from here? First, I recommend taking a break. Go for a walk or check your email. Clear your head because you will want to be fresh for the next chapter on validating assumptions and prioritization.

CHAPTER 3

# ASSUMPTIONS AND PRIORITIZATION

## (BY CODY SIMMS)

*What should I do now and next?*

During his first year with Keller Williams, a real estate agent, David Bain, was named both Keller Williams's International Rookie of the Year and the Austin Board of Realtors Rookie of the Year. I met him in the spring of 2020 when Amos took David through this process. By that time, he had become a very successful agent and was knee deep in the transition from sole proprietor to full-service firm. He and his small staff were overwhelmed with all the work to do. Should they invest in back-office support? How quickly should they hire new agents? When should they approach their own development opportunities? What he needed to know now was where should he focus and, equally as important, what can he ignore?

Together, we started working through these questions along with all the other assumptions he had about his business and the opportunity in front of him. We used the work he had already done with his W3 and revenue formula as a kind of key for prompting and guiding his thoughts, giving him, in his words, "all the things to think about" for the business.

He worked through his potential strategies for where to invest his time, money, and operations using the same skills an expert head of product at a software company would in building their product roadmap and afterward came away with massive clarity he had around where he should (and shouldn't) be spending his time.

I had a lot of fun working with David, particularly because Bain Residential is not a tech business. He never would have thought of the focusing exercise we went through as an exercise in "product prioritization." He certainly wouldn't have known to look to the tools I and others had been using as product leaders in high-growth tech companies over the last two decades. But that is exactly what it was. He started to see not just the service he was providing his customers but also his entire business as a product—a collection of elements that needed to be tested, proven true, and then pushed into the market. My hope is that by the end of this chapter, you will, too.

## STOP PLANNING AND START PRIORITIZING

There may be more books and blog posts on product planning than there are grains of sand on the beaches of Hawaii. And even though I absolutely love Hawaii, I'd prefer to spend my time there surfing the waves rather than digging around in the sand.

Similarly, you should spend your time executing your business rather than fiddling around with your product process or sweating about creating a perfect product roadmap.

Yes, it's hard to find the right chemistry in your company to get product, design, and engineering efforts working in harmony.

There are lots of best practices out there via which to do this (again, the grains of sand thing), but at the end of the day, none of that matters if you aren't bringing the right thing to market in the first place.

Great companies often have great processes, but great processes do not make great companies.

If you aren't building a tech-enabled business, right now, you may be thinking that this chapter isn't relevant for you. But let me stop you right there. What we'll learn here are critical skills of prioritization and assumption validation that apply to any product you are taking to market, whether or not it is a tech-enabled business.

If I can leave you with one key takeaway from this entire chapter, it will be this: great product development comes from having a culture of learning and validation. This is something you can build into your company culture without a lot of process. If you are a tech business, it won't require you to completely rejigger your sprint-planning process, switch from Trello to Asana (or vice versa), or move from kanban to scrum (or vice versa). All of these things are merely implementation details. Although getting these right can certainly help you execute more efficiently, this chapter is not about any of these things.

This chapter is absolutely, positively, *not* about product development processes. It's about product prioritization.

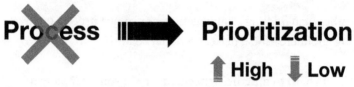

**Process ➡ Prioritization**

⬆ High ⬇ Low

Figure 3.1

You can't afford to waste your time building things that people don't want or won't use. In any business, especially before you hit profitability, time equals runway, and the more time you burn, the more runway you burn, which ends up costing you significantly. Whereas if you spend just a bit more energy up front validating what your customers actually want before trying to build your next great idea, you will end up saving yourself significant time (and thus significant future money).

This chapter is about helping you make sure that you are trying to execute on the right things *before* you spend your precious time and energy doing significant work on them in the first place.

## WHAT IT MEANS TO BE A "PRODUCT PERSON"

We often hear things like "She is a great product person," but what does this mean? Is this person a great user experience designer? Maybe, but usually those kudos would be about her design skills, not product skills. Is she great at getting features through engineering? Possibly, though that's more about velocity and throughput—and thus more of an extension of engineering—than it is about product.

Does it mean that she's good at knowing customer pain points with the product? Most certainly, but eventually, your best customer service folks will share that skill. That doesn't necessarily make them great product folks.

Great product folks, it turns out, pretty much universally excel at asking the right questions about what drives customer behavior and then devising clever ways to find answers to those questions. They are great at (1) having assumptions about their customers' needs, (2) developing hypotheses for testing these assumptions, and (3) prioritizing which of these hypotheses they should test and by when. In many cases, they do all of this intuitively, though they can be learned.

Notice that none of these are things we typically associate with product work, such as running sprint planning, writing requirements or user stories, designing features, or executing roadmaps. Great product people may also be great at these details, too, but mastery of the product implementation process is not what makes someone a great product person. I'll say it again: a great product person has assumptions about their customers' needs, can hypothesize creative ways to satisfy these needs, and can prioritize which hypotheses to test in priority order.

In the early days of your business, the responsibility for doing this work very clearly falls with one of the founders of the company. In fact, it is absolutely imperative. You can't hire out for this.

The founders have to establish this learning and validation culture in the company, because the founders have to be the ones to truly understand the cycle of identifying customer pain points and testing how to solve them.

As a business builder, you are operating in a vast world of unknowns, and the initial steps of trying to make sense of all of the inputs you are getting is why you are building this business. It's on you to make sense of it. Once you have started putting the pieces together and are optimizing your offering to the market rather than defining it, you can start to think about bringing on someone to do these functions; in a typical tech company, that would be a product manager. Until then, it is all on you. Again, that's why you are a founder in the first place. Thus, it's not only important that you learn these "dark art" skills around defining assumptions, developing hypotheses, and prioritizing tests; these are critical factors that will make or break your company.

Maybe you are a natural salesperson. If so, you know how to talk to customers and develop assumptions about their needs, but you may struggle a bit in the leap from assumptions to testable hypotheses. That's okay. It can be learned.

Or maybe you are a 10X engineer or systems-minded person who can solve any technical problem with ease. So you may be good at prioritization and developing solutions, but how do you know you are asking the right questions about what you assume to be driving your customers' behavior? I'll try to address that here, too.

## PRODUCT PRIORITIZATION WORKSHOP

Like Amos's exercises in the previous chapters, this one is quite simple, yet also very hard to get right. You're going to need about an hour or so to do this the first time. So if you don't have it now, earmark this page and come back here when you do.

Additionally, this exercise is much more effective if you do it alongside your leadership team. It does not matter who in the company identifies as a "product person"; you'll want to be inclusive and capture as many inputs and data points as possible as the starting point. You *can* do the first step by yourself, but you'll soon be pooling some of your outputs together and discussing them anyway. So, again, if you cannot work together right now, earmark this page and come back once you and your co-founders have a good hour to devote to this.

Finally, when you do come back, bring a pack of Post-it notes and pens. By default, we're going fully analogue with this one. If you and your team are remote or virtual from one another, you can accomplish the tasks below using a virtual whiteboarding service.[5]

Ready to dive in? Crack open that pack of Post-it notes (or start pulling virtual Post-its out in your virtual whiteboard tool). The instructions are going to be somewhat vague to start, and that's intentional. Please fight through the discomfort in this first step. It will all be worth it.

### STEP 1: WHAT DRIVES YOUR BUSINESS?

Now start to think about the things in the world that you believe drive your business. Think about some of your product plans, tech plans, hiring plans, go-to-market strategies, customer acquisition plans, pricing strategies, competitive ecosystem dynamics, and so forth. Look at the list of drivers from the revenue formula chapter as well.

Don't hold back here.

You're going to take ten minutes to write down one belief statement about what drives your business per Post-it note.

---

5    At the time of this writing, two of the best virtual whiteboarding services are Miro.com and Mural.co.

Don't overthink this. Write as many things as quickly as you can. Ideally, in ten minutes you can have at least twenty Post-it notes, about one every thirty seconds or so. It may feel weird at first, but hopefully you can get in a groove. When you do hit that groove, all of a sudden ten minutes will have passed and you'll still have more you can write. In fact, you may feel like you are just scratching the surface. Maybe you get through go-to-market beliefs and feel like there are still five more rabbit holes you can go down. That's good. Feel free to take an extra few minutes if you have key thoughts still flowing out.

Here are a few random examples to get you started, to show different types of statements for different types of businesses, none of which are related to each other.

I believe the primary channel for customer acquisition will be through organic content marketing.

I believe we should launch our product via university campuses, starting in the midwestern US.

I believe CIOs at Fortune 500 companies want greater transparency into the software that their employees are purchasing via credit card and expense reports.

I believe our primary direct sales channel with be through community events rather than via large account sales.

I believe the initial buyers of our product are engineering managers at growth stage tech startups.

I believe the fear of climate change is influencing where people decide to purchase their first home.

I believe residential real estate agenices are too focused on sales volume and fail to develop leads by offering preparatory services to first-time potential homebuyers before they are ready to buy.

I believe our signup flow is currently the cause of our churn issue.

I believe that, once users have shared three offers via our site, they will become daily active users.

I believe the rise of 5G networks will turn almost every standard industrial device into a remotely hackable machine.

I believe that large enterprises haven't trusted third parties as data intermediaries, but mature decentralized storage technologies is changing this.

I believe it's really hard today to understand how to price residential solar power; consumers want more pricing transparency.

Figure 3.2

For the most part, these are all fairly large and grandiose statements. It's okay to be more nuanced and feature-oriented as well. Again, there is no right or wrong way to do this first step. The most important thing is to write down as many things as possible that you think are factors in what makes your business go.

Having facilitated this exercise with hundreds of companies, the primary place where people get off track during this first exercise is by being too vague in the belief statements. Notice the specificity in my examples above. This is important. This workshop will fail if your initial belief statements are too simplistic. I've seen people write things such as "consumer-friendly user experience" as a belief statement, but this is not an actionable statement. Take the extra fifteen seconds to make each example a true belief statement such as, "I believe that a consumer-friendly user experience helps customers build rapport with our brand."

If you're generally struggling to come up with things, here are two tips:

1. Think about what's on your product roadmap or company priority list today. If you've already prioritized it, presumably you believe it's important.
2. Start to go down pathways of thought. Think about what you believe about pricing and break that down. Then think about what you believe about your competition and why they are lacking from the perspective of your customer. And definitely reference your outputs from the W3 and revenue formula workshops that you did earlier in this book.

Finally, this first exercise is something that every member of your company should do independently. Don't discuss each Post-it as you write it. Go for volume!

Ready? Set a timer for ten minutes and go!

Figure 3.3

Now I'm going to assume that roughly ten minutes have passed, and you have somewhere around twenty belief statements written down per person, or both.

**PAUSE AND REFLECT**

Before we move to step 2, take a minute to think about whether that exercise was easy or hard for you. Did you take a while to get going and then get on a roll? Or did you start fast and then run out of steam? Could you have kept going for another ten minutes? If you feel you really do have a ton more to say, it's totally okay to take some more time and keep going. Or do you still feel lost?

Part of the magic of this workshop is that much like an early-stage business, you are starting this exercise with a whole lot of unknowns in front of you. You know roughly that we're doing a workshop on product prioritization, and you know roughly that I've given you direction to write belief statements (with a few random examples to get you thinking), but you have no idea how this will all come together.

It's a lot like starting a company. You have a rough insight as to why the market might be ready for a new offering, but you don't really know if people want it, how much they'll pay for it, how they'll find it, how you'll find them, if they'll like it, or if it's easy or hard to build.

We're walking through the dark right now, feeling our way around with our hands and feet as much as our eyes, taking in any input we can find. If you've struggled with this exercise, ask yourself whether you struggle working in undefined situations, and if so, know that this is an area you are absolutely going to need to get more comfortable with as you continue to build your business.

Now on to the next step. This is when you'll need to pull your other co-founders (or extended team members) into the exercise, as the rest of this workshop becomes much more effective with a greater volume of data and divergent opinions.

## STEP 2: DO YOU HAVE DATA FOR THAT?

Hopefully, you've wrangled your other team members to do this with you, so it's time to pool all of your Post-it notes together.

If you each did step 1 well, then you've got anywhere from forty to one hundred Post-it notes to read through and discuss, depending on how many of you there are. The more the better.

Talk through each of the notes and make sure you each understand what the others meant when writing it. If you have divergent belief statements, take note of them, but you don't need to resolve that just yet. If you have any that appear to be repeats of each other or are somewhat getting at the same thing, choose just one.

Here's the point of this step: if you have data to back up a belief, draw (or type, if virtual) a big star on the note for it.

Even though this should be an objective question, we're operating in the world of unknowns and many of your belief statements are likely subjective. You're likely going to have lots of debate around whether you have ample data. That's good.

Have those conversations with each Post-it note but remember that you aren't debating whether a statement is true or important. You are merely aiming to agree whether you actually have the data to back up the statement.

Here's the rubric I want you to use as you debate: (1) Do you have some sort of company dashboard that roughly backs up the statement? This could be your analytics engine, your customer relationship management (CRM), your sales data, your customer service logs, what you see in your profit and loss (P&L), or cash flow statement, or your daily customer receipts. Whatever it is, do you have *some* form of primary source data that backs this up, at least at a high level? (2) Have you talked to enough customers such that you truly believe that this statement is true?

Hint: "Enough" means more than one.

In either case, this means you need primary data that you have discovered directly in order to draw a star. If you read it in a market intelligence report, no star. If a prospective investor told you their opinion, no star. This needs to be firsthand data.

Finally, in order to draw that star, ask yourself this: Would I bet Cody $100 that if I show him my data for this sticky, he'd agree with me? In other words, don't overthink this. Your data doesn't need to be so rock solid that you are betting your life savings on it, but you also shouldn't be drawing stars on everything.

Would you bet $100 that a casual observer with no knowledge of your business would agree with you that yes, indeed, you have enough data to justify drawing a star?

Take ten to fifteen minutes (or longer, depending on how many Post-its you have) and make it happen.

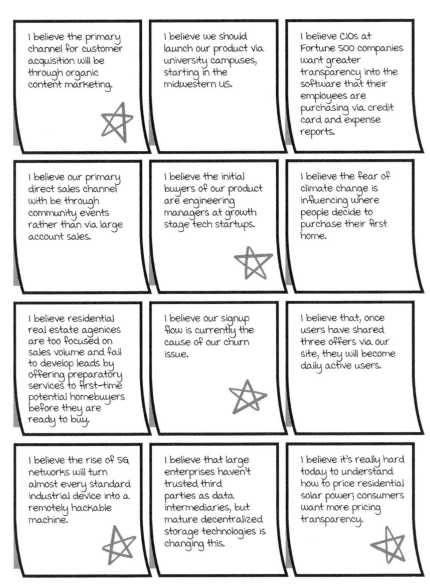

I believe the primary channel for customer acquisition will be through organic content marketing.

I believe we should launch our product via university campuses, starting in the midwestern US.

I believe CIOs at Fortune 500 companies want greater transparency into the software that their employees are purchasing via credit card and expense reports.

I believe our primary direct sales channel with be through community events rather than via large account sales.

I believe the initial buyers of our product are engineering managers at growth stage tech startups.

I believe the fear of climate change is influencing where people decide to purchase their first home.

I believe residential real estate agenices are too focused on sales volume and fail to develop leads by offering preparatory services to first-time potential homebuyers before they are ready to buy.

I believe our signup flow is currently the cause of our churn issue.

I believe that, once users have shared three offers via our site, they will become daily active users.

I believe the rise of 5G networks will turn almost every standard industrial device into a remotely hackable machine.

I believe that large enterprises haven't trusted third parties as data intermediaries, but mature decentralized storage technologies is changing this.

I believe it's really hard today to understand how to price residential solar power; consumers want more pricing transparency.

Figure 3.4

Before we moving on to step 3, ask yourselves what you observed during step 2.

Did you have three or fewer stars? Ten or more stars? There's no right or wrong answer to this question, and one thing that comes up time and time again when I give this workshop is that companies are all over the map.

Sometimes more mature companies have almost no stars, and sometimes less mature companies have quite a few stars. As your business grows, you'll go through ebbs and flows of how much data you have, depending on where you are in a given product rollout cycle.

I once facilitated this exercise in a room that included two to three companies that were little more than a prototype, two to three companies that were somewhere in the ballpark of $50,000–$100,000 in monthly revenue, and one company that had done $20M in sales during the prior year. Believe it or not, the biggest company in the group had one of the lowest star counts. That's because they were entering a new product development cycle and were focusing their effort on the new thing they were building—a product where they knew relatively little about consumer demand.

If you are in the midst of building a new product offering, you may be back to a world of questions and relatively few knowns. If you are in the midst of scaling your first product offering, you may have a less mature business, but because you're in the scaling cycle, you'll generally know what needs to be done to make it successful. In that scenario, your Post-its without data may represent a handful of big future initiatives that you haven't even started working on yet.

Another question worth asking is whether different members of the team approached the exercise in different ways.

Did the CEO have a different train of thought when creating her initial Post-its during step 1 than the head of marketing did? Did the head of sales approach things differently than the head of operations? I often observe that individuals in different functions execute step 1 in very different ways. This of course is a reminder that all of us come into work each day breaking down problems in different ways, and you should never assume that what you are thinking is necessarily in line with how others see things.

You may intuit answers from raw data, whereas others may need a lot more processing time. You may obsess over details, whereas others worry more about existential factors to the business. Hopefully, this diversity is what creates a good team and helps you all see around corners.

One final question worth asking is how did you move ahead when you disagreed? Did the CEO bulldog their opinion through the group? Did you vote? Did you try to force a consensus? Take note of this, as this is your company's decision-making culture in full effect. The culture you create now when your company is small will continue to permeate the business as it grows. These little things matter a lot. Take time to reflect on what you envision your company's decision-making culture to be and what it is in reality.

Now on to step 3.

## STEP 3: WHICH VALIDATED ASSUMPTIONS ARE MOST CRITICAL?

Look at all of your Post-it notes with stars. These are your validated assumptions. These are things that you believe to be drivers of your business and you have the data to back them up.

To do this step, I want you to go through each of these Post-its with stars and think in extremes. Which of these validated beliefs, in their wildest version of success, will drive the next wave of growth for your business? Which of them, if they somehow stop working or stop being true, will end up spelling the end for your business? In either case—where the Post-it will either create wild success or epic failure—I want you to draw a circle around the star.

The rest you can leave alone.

As with every step so far, don't overthink this. Go with your gut. You know what you know. If it feels really important, draw a circle. If it doesn't feel really important, leave it be.

This step shouldn't take you too long—maybe five minutes or so as a team. Go for it. And be conscious around how you make decisions when you have conflict.

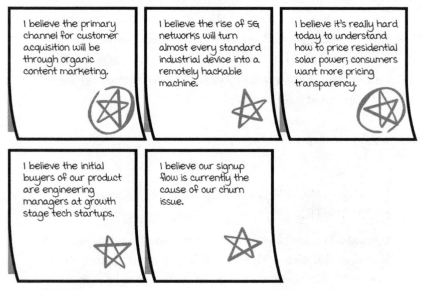

Figure 3.5

Now that you took the time to talk through your validated assumptions and settled on a few of them as the most critical, what did you learn? Were you aligned as a team on which ones were truly important? Was there heavy debate? Are you generally excited and/or worried about the same things as it pertains to the business? Or do you bring different viewpoints into what matters?

All of this is super important. You are each individuals, and you wake up each morning thinking about (or lie in bed at night worried about) different things. One of you may be petrified that you can't get your cost of goods sold to drop by another 10 percent, whereas another of you may be much more worried about what Tesla is going to announce next in the march to vehicle autonomy. Be aware of this diversity of thought. When you come into work each morning, take a deep breath before declaring something to be a critical priority. Keep in mind that each of you may be thinking about different things. If you are totally aligned on what you care about, even better. Now, how do you make sure you aren't missing anything?

You can probably guess where this is going in step 4.

### STEP 4: WHICH UNVALIDATED ASSUMPTIONS ARE MOST CRITICAL?

This time, look at all of your sticky notes without stars. These are your unvalidated assumptions. They are things about your business that you believe to be true, although in actuality, you really don't know.

Which of these unvalidated assumptions are most critical to your business?

You are clearly guessing here since you don't have real data, but you can use step 3's rubric about thinking in extremes to answer this question. Which ones look like they would either unlock the next wave of massive growth or, if they stop working, will cause your business to fall off a cliff? In the cases where you feel a given Post-it note represents one of these extremes, draw a circle on it. Put the rest aside.

This should be a relatively quick exercise. Take five minutes or so for it.

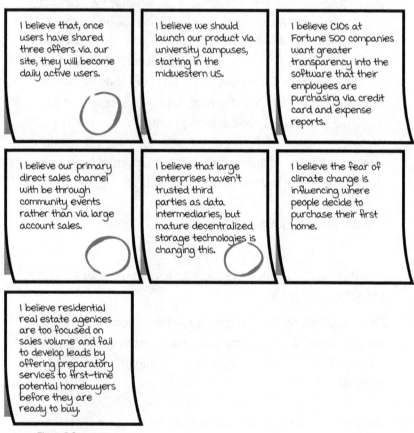

Figure 3.6

Anything stand out? Any big aha moments for the team? This is the step where many businesses will realize that some of their most foundational beliefs about the business are in fact not validated. And that's okay. In fact, that's great. That's what you want to figure out by doing this.

I find that this step is also often where pet projects tend to fall below the priority line. Each of us has ideas about things that could possibly move the needle for the business that we think are important. It's only when seeing them alongside other truly mission critical items and having to make choices about priority that we often realize these things just aren't as important as we may have initially thought.

Don't waste time. Go figure out how to create hypotheses around each of these beliefs and get validating.

### STEP 5: FOUR PILES OF POST-ITS

You now have four piles of Post-it notes you can use for road-mapping and planning:

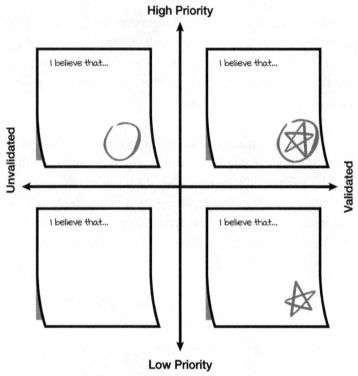

Figure 3.7

*High-Priority Validated Assumptions (Circle + Star)*

Figure 3.8

This broad swath of stuff is where you should be operationalizing. This is what's ready for you to productize and execute on. These are things that you believe to be true, you have data that says it is true, and you believe it to be important. This is your core.

Note that individual features (by that I mean what customers actually experience with your product) should still go through feature validation, which is like a mini version of this whole exercise. More on that in a bit. But you've at least got your North Star here.

*High-Priority Unvalidated Assumptions (Circle, No Star)*

Figure 3.9

You URGENTLY need to address these items. These are items that you believe to be critical drivers of your business, yet in actuality, you really have no idea. You are guessing. These items should absolutely be keeping you up at night. They could unlock the next wave of growth, or they could spell imminent doom. Don't ignore things in this list. Rather, start building a plan around breaking these items down into bite-sized hypotheses and figuring out how to get some real data that could help you understand if each of these things is actually real. Begin prioritizing ways to validate these assumptions ASAP. Because if these things aren't true or don't work, you'll need to create some contingencies and fast. These items are the most important part of this whole exercise.

*Low-Priority Validated Assumptions (No Circle, Star)*

I believe that...

Figure 3.10

These are items you believe drive your business and you have data to back it up, but you also don't believe they are critically important to the business. Deprioritize work here relative to the higher priority items above.

Some of this may be maintenance work. Some of it may just be project work that you feel you need to do, but force yourself to ask the hard questions about the relative importance of these items rather than the more critical path items. If an item is below the line in terms of priority, there is no reason to spend considerable time there.

*Low-Priority Unvalidated Assumptions (No Circle, No Star)*

I believe that...

Figure 3.11

Much like the items immediately above this one, these things are likely less important to spend time on. Now, there's some risk here, as you don't *really* know since, in fact, these items are unvalidated. But you have to trust your gut somewhere, and these feel like they are less important than the high-priority unvalidated items. You have to draw a line somewhere.

## FEATURE-LEVEL PRIORITIZATION

As I mentioned in the lead-in, this is not a product planning exercise. It's not helping you take features through sprint planning. That's a totally different type of exercise. Rather, it is a prioritization exercise. Hopefully, it helped you to see where the big glaring holes are in what you know about your business, your market, your product, and your customers. And that's incredibly valuable insight.

Many companies are trying to move so fast that they sometimes forget to stop to ask themselves these questions. Taking the time to make sure you aren't building your whole business on a house of cards (those unvalidated assumptions) is slowing down to speed up.

You can also use this same exercise at the individual feature level. What do you know? What do you not know? What's critical? What's not critical? You can use that information to decide what to take through feature validation.

## CREATING HYPOTHESES TO TEST YOUR ASSUMPTIONS

There still is more to the dark art of product that I mentioned in my introduction—namely, how do you develop hypotheses to test your assumptions? This is aligned with doing the Post-it note exercise at the individual feature level, and it is another skill that takes time to develop.

It's relatively easy to come up with a feature and build or offer it to the market. It's much harder to come up with a well-written hypothesis that you want to test, then force yourself to write down ten to fifteen possible tests you could run to validate or invalidate that hypothesis. But that's how you start to develop a truly agile and iterative product development process. If you can run those tests and validate those hypotheses without actually building and shipping features or spending tons of money, then super kudos to you. Maybe you can then invalidate some of the hypotheses with customer interviews, or with some lightweight design prototype user research, or by trying something light-weight in a different part of your product. Get creative and try to be as resourceful as you can.

You will be amazed how much you can learn by offering customers a $25 gift card for thirty minutes of their time to provide you with specific insights on a key question you have. Recruit customers to participate in insight sessions via a survey on your website, an email blast, or by soliciting them in person. Use your W3 to try to narrow down the prospective insight providers to just customers who fit your target profile. Then develop methods for getting structured insight from them. This could be a set of interview questions you ask them; this could be by having them attempt to use your product and observing where they struggle. If you can afford to hire a user experience researcher to help you glean these insights, go for it. But stay deeply involved in the process. Again, this is not something you can just hire out for. You need to get your hands dirty here and truly understand your customers' needs, desires, and frustrations.

I'm often asked how you can know when you have enough data. I don't believe there's a black or white answer to this. What hypothesis are you trying to validate, and how many tests have you run to try to validate this hypothesis? Are you learning something totally different with each test? Or are you generally learning the same thing?

Yes, there's a risk that you could be unlucky and hit multiple false positives in a row, but sometimes in the early stages of your business, you have to let good enough be good enough and just go for it. You didn't *fully* jump off a ledge. You ran multiple tests to try to validate a theory, and you generally felt like you were making an informed decision. So go for it.

I'm also often asked if all of this is really necessary. To some, taking the time to ask whether an assumption has been validated and running tests to validate hypotheses feels like an overly conservative way to run a business. To some, it feels risk averse. I can see how one could interpret things that way, but I disagree wholeheartedly.

All founders have taken on massive risk simply by pursuing their business in the first place. It would be much easier to go somewhere and take a job with a salary, bonus, and benefits, but where's the impact in that? At the same time, we don't need to compound that risk by jumping off a ledge of hope every single time we pursue a new initiative or prioritize a new feature. The best entrepreneurs are actually ones who out-execute the competition by being faster at validating what the market wants than anyone else. They reduce waste and don't spend multiple cycles building a product no one wants or trying to sell something that no one wants to buy. They attack the market with purpose and with clear intent, which is to learn faster than anyone else out there and then step on the gas pedal once they have clear insight into customer demand or into a feature that will increase growth.

## BUILD A ROADMAP

The last note I will leave you with on this overall topic is that every company has to have a roadmap, a picture of where the business is headed. If not to run the day-to-day product, then at least to share with your staff, potential investors, future investors, board members, new hires, and so forth. Folks want to know where you (think you) are heading.

I can't tell you how many times I've seen roadmaps that clearly were created in order to fit the right number of items onto a balanced-looking slide rather than ones that were grounded in what the business needs to actually solve. I know I've been guilty of this myself in the earlier days of my own product journey. "Oooh, this slide looks imbalanced. There are an uneven number of initiatives in Q3 and Q4 compared to Q1 and Q2, so let's move an item from Q2 to Q3. Or let's add a new thing into Q4. No one will remember by the time we get to Q4 that we said we were going to do that thing anyway."

**Product Roadmap**

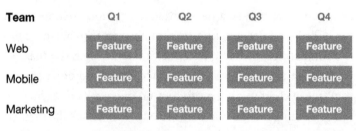

| Team | Q1 | Q2 | Q3 | Q4 |
|---|---|---|---|---|
| Web | Feature | Feature | Feature | Feature |
| Mobile | Feature | Feature | Feature | Feature |
| Marketing | Feature | Feature | Feature | Feature |

Figure 3.12

This is not good.

So what is a *good* roadmap?

Is it a sacred blueprint of everything the business plans to execute? No. The notion of a roadmap as a long-term blueprint of product features has its roots in the early days of software development when software was printed on CD-ROMs and sold in retail stores such as Best Buy and CompUSA. You needed to know what features were going to be in the next version of the software with enough lead time to build the product, get it physically burned onto a CD, get the packaging done (including bullet-pointed lists of features) and get it onto trucks in order to hit a release date that was coordinated with marketing. With the slight exception of deeply complex hardware products, we just don't develop products this way in 2020.

Is a roadmap an aspirational plan that shows what you *hope* to achieve in the business by a certain date? Maybe, as long as you set clear expectations that your roadmap will shift as you gain market feedback. The challenge with this is that when you course correct and shift plans according to market feedback, you have to reeducate your stakeholders on your new plan. This creates challenges in expectation setting and can start to create a perception that your plan is constantly changing, when in fact you are doing the right thing by reacting nimbly to what the market is saying. In this case, why go through the effort of the initial feature roadmap when it will end up just causing you more work?

I'm a big believer in creating a "learning roadmap." You have to communicate to your stakeholders where you'll be spending your resources and where you are trying to go. But rather than being defined by features and dates, your learning roadmap defines the assumptions you want to validate and the dates by when you need to validate them. It's a prioritized view of the things assumed to be most critical to the company, from subject to test.

Some of this is semantics. It's the difference between saying "Shipping project X by Y date is critical to the company. We will put all hands on deck!" (bad) versus "We believe that we need to figure out whether X is important or not by Y date. We are putting our best resources toward testing our assumptions. If we do find out it's important, then we plan to have product in market around this area by Z date" (good).

It's a little more complex to do things this way, but if you orient your stakeholders around dates by which you want to learn whether something matters as opposed to dates by which you want to ship features, you help create that culture of learning and validation in your company.

**Learning Roadmap**

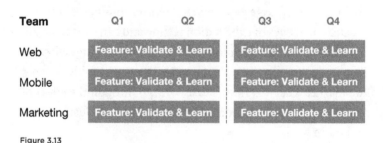

Figure 3.13

This learning roadmap aligns really well with today's agile and lean startup product development methodologies.

In the past, when developing product to get a CD-ROM on a truck, the waterfall style, the name for a linear approach to designing, building, and shipping products was appropriate. You needed to optimize for having a finite set of features to be complete by a set date that was often months or quarters away. Product roadmaps were actually signed off by sales, marketing, engineering, QA, design, and so on, and then the product went from product management to design to engineering to QA to production in a straight line. That's why it was called waterfall.

In today's interconnected world, we can get customer feedback in parallel with product development. This has led to a product development world where we can have deeper confidence that what we're building today will resonate with customers but with much less fidelity on what exactly we may be building two quarters from now. And that's okay.

For some reason, our roadmapping process today still tends to be more of a waterfall-looking document, but it doesn't have to be. Rather than defining arbitrary things we hope to ship two quarters from now, we can define what we hope to learn two quarters from now—what's really important to know about our business in the future—and how we plan to learn it.

All of this holds true at the feature level as well. Stop thinking about prioritizing features and start thinking about prioritizing assumptions that need to be validated. As I said previously, I believe the biggest risk founders take is the day they start their business. From then on, the best founders are the ones who out-execute the market by reducing waste and being faster than anyone else at figuring out what the market wants.

Remember, if you don't have data, you only have hope. And

you aren't taking on the risk of entrepreneurship because you hope it is going to work. Hope isn't a strategy. Your goal as a founder is to put as much in your own control as possible. If you get good at data-led planning, you gain a much greater hit rate when developing successful offerings that the market wants.

## CREATING LEARNING-FOCUSED RHYTHMS

One final word of advice that I give to companies is to look at ways you can use some of the principles above and build daily and weekly rhythms. The workshop above isn't something you'd do on a weekly basis, although I do think it's a helpful way to take a step back once a quarter or so. But on a daily basis, you can still bring learning into your daily standup practices.

What if every member of the company were asked to create a daily learning goal and to report on what you learned during standup along with blockers and tasks? What if this learning goal is something that each person can do in fifteen minutes or less and could be achieved on their own without the help of another team member?

For someone in marketing, perhaps this is taking fifteen minutes each day to look at various analytics dashboards or funnel reports and finding a new insight to share. For someone in sales, perhaps this is asking one additional question about the competitive landscape on your sales calls that day and reporting back on your learnings. For someone in product or design, maybe this is going through a clean onboarding flow of someone else's product and learning how they are handling customer activation. For someone in engineering, maybe this is looking at customer service feedback and deducing where people are getting stuck somewhere in your product.

Whatever it is, if everyone in the company spends fifteen minutes each day establishing and executing on a learning goal and reporting on it in the next day's standup, you'll be amazed at how much knowledge you'll develop about your business.

There are also ways you can make this an even deeper part of the fabric of the company.

What if you took this same principle but instead made a weekly learning goal at the company level—something that the entire company will rally around learning that week. What if 10 percent of the product hours you assign in your weekly sprint planning exercises were allocated to this company learning goal? This would mean that 10 percent of your company's resources would be focused on learning a critical new aspect of your business that week, and you'd report on the results during your weekly all-hands or KPI meeting. If you did that, you'd very quickly have a backlog of things you'd want to learn, and you'd in essence start to have a learning backlog!

On that note, it's time for the next chapter from Trevor on how to create KPIs for your business that truly become your business dashboard.

## CHAPTER 4

# KEY PERFORMANCE INDICATORS

## (BY TREVOR BOEHM)

*Is what I'm doing working?*

Oluwasoga ("Soga") Oni and his three co-founders have a big vision: to provide high-quality and affordable care for Africa's next billion people. They launched MDaaS, a network of private diagnostic facilities in 2015. When I met them in 2018, they had reached a major milestone toward that vision—launching their first center in Nigeria—but the journey to get there had been anything but straightforward. The company didn't begin as a network of facilities. Originally, MDaaS started as a medical equipment supplier, but they couldn't get traction beyond the wealthy hospitals in the country. Then they shifted to leasing the medical equipment but ran into the same problem: only wealthy hospitals were interested. "During all this iteration, there were some low points when things weren't working, and you realize your baby is ugly," Soga later wrote in an interview with FINCA Ventures, one of their investors. "But we just persisted."

Soga, more than almost any CEO I've met, has a relentless commitment to search the data to find what's working. As he kept pushing through, he pored over the numbers in his business—which customers had said yes, which said no, and where his inbound requests for medical equipment were coming from. The team also started talking to customers, interviewing them to better understand why they were or weren't buying. They figured out that they weren't seeing growth because the problem wasn't just a lack of access to quality medical equipment; it was a lack of quality diagnostic services generally. Doctors just didn't have reliable places to send their patients to get the right diagnostics. So MDaaS decided to take it on themselves to build and operate those diagnostic centers. After that, suddenly, things started working.

## FINDING WHAT WORKS

The goal of this chapter is to help you know if the things you are doing in your business are working, and more importantly, whether those things matter in the first place. By the end of it, you will have a single core metric that you track as a company that can align and focus your efforts as a team. You'll also have a clear milestone or goal for where you want that metric to be in the future. To make sure each team knows how to measure their own progress, you'll also choose one key metric to track for each team, along with any supporting metrics you want to track to make sure everything in the business is staying healthy. Together, these will make up your key performance indicators (KPIs). Finally, you'll create a plan for how and when you will engage with those metrics.

You can expect the entire process to take a few hours, and you'll want to include each member of your leadership team in the discussion. You can complete it from start to finish in one setting, but really, it's best used as a starting point for a few key conversations across your business—beginning with leadership and the teams they lead.

## WHAT ARE KPIS ANYWAY?

I like to think about metrics as a language. They communicate things about what happened in your business in the past, what's happening now, and what might be happening in the future. They are a numerical way of answering questions about what's happening in your business. KPIs are answers to the most important questions.

KPIs matter because they give you a data-driven way to make decisions about what to do in your business. They help you understand whether something you tried worked—if it helped you get closer to where you're trying to move as a business.

**KPIs are decision-making tools.** They are only useful to the degree that they help you decide what to actually do in your business.

They also keep you intellectually honest as a business builder. They keep you from lying to yourself that something is working when it's not.

There is no blanket template for which KPIs you should use in your business. But there are questions you can ask yourself in order to uncover the right KPIs for your business at this specific moment in time. After working with hundreds of companies, I've discovered there are three fundamental questions that, if you can answer, you'll be well on your way to finding KPIs.

Here they are:

- What's the single most important thing we have to achieve as a business right now? Why does that thing matter? How will you know you've achieved it?
- What number tells us the status of that thing—whether what we are trying right now is helping us get there or not?
- Once we've achieved that most important thing, what will it enable us to achieve next?

I'll spend the rest of this chapter unpacking each of these questions and how you can use them to find and use your KPIs.

Before I do, though, it's best to take ten minutes and write down each question for yourself.

Each member of your leadership team should answer independently—don't work together or share your answers. When you're done, take another ten minutes to share together as a leadership team what you wrote. As you do, don't try to get to a shared set of answers; just share what you have and any reflections you have on the exercise and on what each of you said. Once you're done with this part, you can work through the rest of the chapter collaboratively as a team and align to one collective answer as you do.

Are your answers written down? Have you shared them with your team?

Good. Let's unpack each question, one by one.

## QUESTION 1: THE MOST IMPORTANT THING

What's the single most important thing we have to achieve as a business right now? Why does that thing matter?

This is obviously a big question and one that can be difficult to answer in a metrics-driven way. But the good news is, if you've done the previous work in this book, with just a little bit of thinking, the answer will start to become obvious.

Here's what I mean:

- What do you know about your W3?
- What do you know about your revenue formula?
- What do you know about your assumptions?

If we think of the revenue formula as a theory for how the business makes money, each driver actually represents a different (unvalidated) assumption. Let's walk through an example to show what I mean using MDaaS from the start of the chapter.

As a reminder, MDaaS is a network of diagnostic and primary care facilities across Africa. Their revenue formula is depicted in figure 4.1, where "# of Centers" are the number of facilities MDaaS has around the world. "Average Visits per Center" are the number of monthly visits at each center. "Conversion" is the percentage of those visitors who become patients, and "Average Price per Visit" is the average revenue each patient generated during their visit.

## This is MDaaS's revenue formula

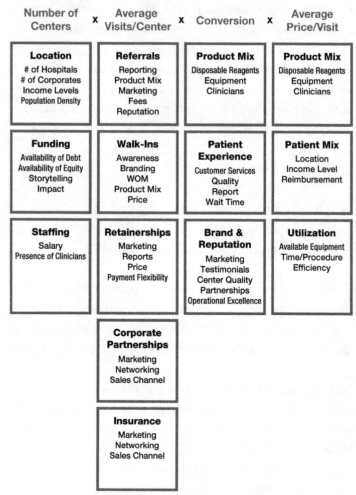

| Number of Centers | x | Average Visits/Center | x | Conversion | x | Average Price/Visit |
|---|---|---|---|---|---|---|
| **Location**<br>\# of Hospitals<br>\# of Corporates<br>Income Levels<br>Population Density | | **Referrals**<br>Reporting<br>Product Mix<br>Marketing<br>Fees<br>Reputation | | **Product Mix**<br>Disposable Reagents<br>Equipment<br>Clinicians | | **Product Mix**<br>Disposable Reagents<br>Equipment<br>Clinicians |
| **Funding**<br>Availability of Debt<br>Availability of Equity<br>Storytelling<br>Impact | | **Walk-Ins**<br>Awareness<br>Branding<br>WOM<br>Product Mix<br>Price | | **Patient Experience**<br>Customer Services<br>Quality<br>Report<br>Wait Time | | **Patient Mix**<br>Location<br>Income Level<br>Reimbursement |
| **Staffing**<br>Salary<br>Presence of Clinicians | | **Retainerships**<br>Marketing<br>Reports<br>Price<br>Payment Flexibility | | **Brand & Reputation**<br>Marketing<br>Testimonials<br>Center Quality<br>Partnerships<br>Operational Excellence | | **Utilization**<br>Available Equipment<br>Time/Procedure<br>Efficiency |
| | | **Corporate Partnerships**<br>Marketing<br>Networking<br>Sales Channel | | | | |
| | | **Insurance**<br>Marketing<br>Networking<br>Sales Channel | | | | |

Figure 4.1

Using real math, MDaaS revenue formula plays out like this (assuming these numbers are tracked over a month):

1 Center × 700 visits × 90 percent conversion to patients × $23 per visit = $14,490 per month

Now let's walk through each top-line value and reframe them as a belief statement or assumption about the business.

Number of centers can become something like, "We believe we can scale across multiple geographies." Average visits per center can be, "We believe we can get people to come to the clinic." Conversion from visit to patient can become, "We believe we can serve them with care that matches their needs." And price can be something like, "We believe we can earn a high enough price per patient to make money."

Once you start seeing your revenue formula in this way, you can ask yourself which of these drivers (or subdrivers) represents the most critical, unvalidated assumption. Ask yourself, "What is the thing that's most likely going to kill me right now if I don't get it right?"

For MDaaS, we're going to say this is average visits per center (phrased as question: "Can we get people in the door?"). Now that we have decided that is our most critical, unvalidated assumption, we can ask ourselves a different question: "Of all the things I can do to move that variable, where do I have the most leverage?" In other words, where do I believe (subject to testing) if I apply the most amount of effort I'm going to get the best results?

You can look through your subdrivers to find the answer. For MDaaS, they discovered this answer was referrals. They believed (subject to testing) the best way to get people in the door is through referrals and that not getting people in the door would kill the business. MDaaS had found their most important thing and the place to focus their efforts.

Now you can get even more granular by zooming in on a sub-

subdriver. These are where your actual experiments live—the concrete things you'll test each week to try to move your core metric.

Hopefully, you are starting to see the power of how these concepts, when put together, allow you to ladder up and down from the most strategic aspects of your business to the most tactical. And it also, by default, gives you your top-line KPIs.

By literally copy/pasting your weekly numbers from the revenue formula and zooming in the one that's most critical to prove right now, you already have the basics of your company's KPIs. Figure 4.2 shows an example using MDaaS.

| | | | |
|---|---|---|---|
| *Can we get patients to show up?*<br>**200** (+10%)<br>**Visits per Week** | | | **70%** (+2%)<br>**Visitor-to-Patient Conversion** |
| | | | *Can we earn enough per visit?*<br>**$30** (12%)<br>**Revenue per Patient** |
| **150**<br>(+30%)<br>Through<br>Referrals | **20**<br>(–5%)<br>Through<br>Walk-Ins | **30**<br>(+10%)<br>Through<br>Corporate | *Can we scale?*<br>**1**<br>Center |

Figure 4.2

Are these the final KPIs you'll settle on to help you understand what's happening in your business and what to do about it? Maybe or maybe not. You'll find out as you use them. But it gives you a place to start that's rooted in the work you've done already.

Now take ten minutes to work with your team to explore your

answer further and align on a single answer. Here are a few more questions to discuss as you do:

- What's the single most important thing we have to achieve as a business right now? Why does that thing matter?
- Where does the thing we most need to achieve live in the revenue formula? What driver(s) does it affect?
- What will achieving this goal prove about our W3?
- What validated, high-priority assumptions are we acting on with this focus?
- What unvalidated, high-priority assumptions are we trying to prove with this focus?
- What number tells us the status of that thing, whether what we are trying is working?

**QUESTION 2: ARE WE GETTING THERE?**

**What number tells us the status of that thing—whether what we are trying right now is helping us get there or not?**

This is where we start to unpack what I call KPI or metrics *hygiene.* You can also consider it a kind of glossary of metrics. These are my definitions, and you'll find slightly different ones in different places. Use this as a reference, but don't feel like you have to memorize or understand everything. What matters most is that you understand what you're measuring and why. At the end, I've included a simple heuristic for which types of metrics tend to work better as KPIs.

### INPUTS AND OUTPUTS

One simple way to understand your metrics is by categorizing them as inputs or outputs.

*Inputs: Things that You Do*
*You control these directly.*

Inputs measure effort. Examples of inputs are number of emails sent, number of sales meetings conducted, number of lines of code written, and average response times to customer support requests. Inputs are useful to track to keep people accountable (*Did Joe actually make the calls he said he would? Did this experiment not turn out the way we thought because our assumptions were wrong or because we failed to execute?*), but they don't tell you anything about the impact their work had.

*Outputs: Things that Happen as a Result of What You Do*
*You can't control these directly, but you can affect them.*

Examples are revenue, active user growth, customer churn, and customer acquisition cost. The most useful metrics for startups are outputs, but sometimes inputs are all you have to measure in the immediate term.

## LAGGING INDICATORS AND LEADING INDICATORS
Lagging and leading indicators help you understand how actionable your metrics are.

*Lagging Indicators: Measure What Already Happened*
Lagging indicators are numbers that only move after a bunch of other things have already happened. They are slow to change. The percentage of customers that churn or number of completed transactions are examples of likely lagging indicators because they only happen after and as a result of a lot of other activity in the business.

*Leading Indicators: Measure What Might Be Happening*

Leading indicators are numbers that move early and that help you predict where other things in the business might be going. Customer engagement metrics, such as number of minutes spent in your app, can be an example of a leading indicator for customer churn. If customers stop using your product, they are much more likely to stop paying for your product. As another example, number of visits to your website, might be a leading indicator of completed transactions because in order to complete a transaction, a person has to first visit your website.

You'll notice that metrics can only be leading or lagging in relation to each other.

## COUNTS, TOTALS, RATES, AND RATIOS

Knowing whether a number is a count, total, rate, or ratio will help you see what kind of insights you can and can't get from your metrics.

### Counts

Counts are tallies of something that's happened over a certain time period: This week, thirty new users signed up; we sent six outreach emails; we ate 231 donuts.

They can be helpful in tracking your progress on how well you're executing a task, but they don't tell you much of anything about where you're headed.

### Totals

Totals are a cumulation of a number over time: Since the start of the business, we have sold 5,000 products; we had one million users download our app; we ate 1,561 donuts. The fast food restaurant McDonald's used to have "Over 99 billion served" on their signs.

Totals can help you see how close or far away you are from a goal or milestone. They can give you a sense of scale, position, or orientation. They're great for puff pieces, but they do nothing to measure the growth rate in a company. *Lean Startup* author Eric Ries calls these "vanity metrics." Generally, stay away from these.

### Rates

Rates are a measure of how fast things are happening: We're growing 10 percent in revenue week over week.

Rates help you see into the future. Especially when combined with historical data (a four-week trailing average, for instance), they can tell you a lot about the trajectory of your business.

### Ratios

Ratios are a measure of the relationship of one thing to another: Fifty percent of all of our users are active (post at least once a day).

They can tell you all kinds of insights you wouldn't be able to see otherwise. They are numbers put into context. They can serve as health checks in the business and help you discover inflection points that you can exploit later.

## A FEW RULES OF THUMB

The best metrics clearly tell you what's working and what's not and then help you do something about it. If you want a simple heuristic, here are some general rules:

- Choose metrics that show you where opportunities or dangers might be arising (leading, not lagging).
- Choose metrics that indicate real progress, not just the effort you're spending (outputs, not inputs).
- Choose metrics that give you a sense of the model—how each part of the business fits into the whole (rates and ratios, just counts and totals).

| | WHAT IT IS | EXAMPLES | CAR ANALOGY | WHAT THEY CAN DO |
|---|---|---|---|---|
| **COUNTS** | A tally of **what's happened** over a period of time | • 10 orders<br>• $10k MRR<br>• $25k monthly cash burn | 150 miles on trip odometer | • Measures incremental progress<br>• Keeps team accountable |
| **TOTALS** | A **cumulation** of a number over time | • 10,000 medication reviews<br>• 10,000 downloads<br>• $66.57 cash on hand | 100,000 miles on car odometer; 1/4 gas left in tank | • Offers a sense of scale, position, and orientation<br>• Feeds your ego |
| **RATES** | A measure of **how fast** things are happening | 10% weekly growth in daily active users | 50 MPH | • Helps you see where you might be going and when |
| **RATIOS** | A measure of **relationship** of one thing to another | • % of listings that are active<br>• % of users that have >3 connections | 25 MPG | • Drives insights<br>• Serves as a health check |

Figure 4.3

Now take ten minutes to revisit the second question to align on a single answer as a team. As you do, think about these questions:

- What number tells us the status of that thing, whether what we are trying is working?
- How sensitive is our number? Does it reveal potential opportunities or dangers quickly and clearly, or will it take some time for us to pick up the signal?
- Does the core metric have the right context to be useful? Which time periods do we want to compare it to (per day, per week, per month, or seasonally)?
- Are we measuring effort that reflects work done or outcomes that reflect actual progress? If effort, what should we do to ensure that effort is having the intended effect?

## QUESTION 3: WHAT'S NEXT?

Once we've achieved that "most important thing," what will it enable us to achieve next?

To understand the power of this question, it's best to start with a story.

Say you're walking along one day and you see a mountain in the distance. You decide you want to climb it. But right now, you can't because the mountain and you are quite a distance apart. In order to be able to climb the mountain, you've got to walk to it. So you get started.

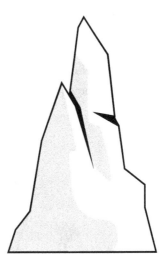

Figure 4.4

You're a pretty experienced trekker, so as you go, you know that you need to pay attention to two key things: (1) the direction you're going and (2) how fast you're walking. These become your KPIs. If you don't walk toward the mountain, that's bad. You'll never get to your goal. And if you go too slow, you won't get there before dark. That's bad, too.

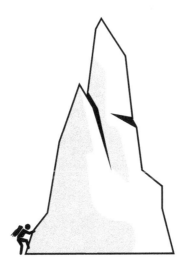

Figure 4.5

Thankfully, you keep heading straight and your speed is fast enough that you make it before the sun goes down. Now you're in a new reality. Before you started walking, climbing wasn't even a possibility; now it is. It's time to get climbing.

Figure 4.6

Your new goal is to climb up, and a new set of things are important to you: (1) having enough anchor points in the rock so you don't fall and die and (2) going up fast enough. These are your new KPIs.

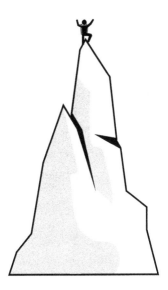

Figure 4.7

Thankfully, you're a pretty good climber, too, and you make it! Your first goal set you up to be able to reach the bigger goal, which itself can become a setup for another goal, such as base jumping.

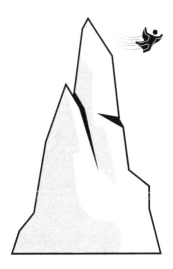

Figure 4.8

So what does all this mean?

1. Your KPIs are relative—they only matter to the degree that they help you see whether you're getting to a key milestone.
2. Milestones are just steps along the "if this, then that" chain.
3. The value of a milestone is in its ability to make a new milestone possible. They only matter to the degree that change the fundamental reality your business operates in so you can do new things.

In other words:

If this...

...then that.

If that...

...then this.

Figure 4.9

Now take ten minutes to revisit the third question to align on a single answer as a team. As you do, think about these questions:

- Once we've achieved that "most important thing," what will it enable us to achieve next?
- How will we know we've achieved our most important thing? What milestone will our core metric hit?
- Describe the new reality we'll be in once we achieve our most important thing. What other metrics will change and how?
- How many steps down the "if this, then that; if that, then…" logic chain have we thought through?
- What metric might we focus on to tell us whether we're getting closer to achieving the next most important thing?

## SETTING KPIS FOR EACH TEAM OR DEPARTMENT

Now that you have clarity as a company around where you're trying to go, you can take these same questions and have your leaders work with their teams to align on a core metric and set of KPIs for each of their teams. Here are the same questions, with one added to encourage alignment with their goals and the overall company goals:

- What's the single most important thing we have to achieve as a team right now? Why does it matter?
- How does that thing impact the overall growth of the business? Where does it live in the revenue formula? How does it support the company-wide core metric we just set? (It's okay if it does so indirectly.)
- What number tells us the status of that thing—whether what we are trying right now is helping us get there or not?

- Once we've achieved that "most important thing," what will it enable us to achieve next?

## PUTTING YOUR KPIS INTO PRACTICE

Once you start on the path of identifying the numbers you'll be tracking, the next key challenge will be embedding them into everyday culture and decision making. If your entire team is not using the metrics you came up with to actually decide what to do in the business, the exercise is useless.

As a core leadership team, and with any team leads or department heads, answer each of these questions:

- **Where will our KPIs live?** The more accessible the better. You might keep them on a TV screen in your office or written on a whiteboard. Everyone should know where they can go to see where your KPIs are right now and where they've been over time.
- **Who on the team will own the process of tracking KPIs?** Although everyone will be accountable to their individual metrics, it's helpful to have a single person who is responsible for setting up the "instrumentation" or process and tools you use to capture and present your KPIs.
- **What will our process be for running experiments to figure out how to move our KPIs predictably?** Remember, KPIs are decision-making tools. To best use them as such, you'll need to build a culture and process for running experiments as a company to figure out what moves those KPIs. Experiments are about creating a disciplined process around finding what works in your business. They start with a question or a belief, and then that question or belief is refined into a quantifiable (disprovable) hypothesis. Then

you do something to see if you were right or wrong, and you take what happened and try to understand why. Now, here comes the most important part: you take that why and form a new question or belief out of it so that whatever you do next builds on the learning you just had.

- **When and how will we check in on them regularly?** Start with running a weekly KPI meeting where you review the company KPIs and each team talks through the status of their key metric and the experiments they ran to try to move it. During these meetings, focus on answering four questions: (1) What did you do to move the KPI? (2) What happened? (3) Why do you think it happened? (4) What will you do next as a result?

- **When will we do a longer deep dive on these numbers? Who should be involved?** Create space once a quarter or even once a month to discuss as a team broader trends you might notice within your metrics. Spend time reviewing the goals you set for that time period, where your numbers have been going, and how the KPIs you've chosen have or haven't helped you reach those goals.

- **Are there any other metrics we should be watching on a daily, weekly, or monthly basis? Why?** There may be metrics you didn't discuss going through this exercise that you may not be trying to move directly but you want to make sure you keep an eye on. Make sure to capture those as a team now and include them.

I've yet to meet a company that didn't struggle, at least at first, to identify the right KPIs for their business. But by building on the work you've already done in this book, you will begin to form a cohesive understanding of not only what needs to happen next but also how to measure whether it's happening. As you keep testing, that understanding will eventually grow into a fully formed model, giving you insights not only into what's happening now but ultimately giving you the ability to predict what's happening in the future. That's where we're headed next.

**CHAPTER 5**

# FINANCIAL MODELING

## (BY TROY HENIKOFF)

*What's my plan?*

Meggie Williams is always up for doing the hard work.

So much so that she decided to build and launch a pet and pet parent social destination—complete with daycare, dog-walking, a dog park, and a bar—in the middle of a pandemic.

Skiptown was a vision born out of thousands of customer interactions and a deep intimacy with the data in the business. Meggie had started her original business, Skipper, years before as an on-demand dog-walking service. At that time, they had two big competitors, and in the following months, those two competitors raised hundreds of millions of dollars and started to move much faster than Skipper was able to. However, Skipper had a couple of things that those two companies didn't (and still don't) have, including a strong handle on their reason for being, a strong belief in using data and metrics to guide their vision, and an equally strong belief that positive unit economics will beat out blind growth in the long term. A few major insights—guided by the same processes laid out this book—led the team to a big bet: building out a 24,000 square foot dog park and bar that would serve as the hub for all their pet-related services. Here's an excerpt from the email Meggie sent to her investors just four weeks after they opened:

> *Despite the ongoing COVID-19 pandemic and associated customer behavior changes and government restrictions, we're seeing great indicators of future success on both the bar/social and pet care sides of our business.*
>
> *1. **Opening dog boarding**—and beating September's projected boarding usage and revenue in just its first weekend in operation.*
>
> *2. **Boarding revenue growth putting us 4.5x ahead** of September's boarding revenue projections despite being less than halfway through the month.*
>
> *3. **Driving daycare visits and getting 30 percent ahead of pace** for daycare revenue.*
>
> *4. **Keeping bar and social personnel costs 60 percent lower** by focusing on the bottom line.*
>
> *5. **Exceeding bar attendance projections by 8 percent for people and 27 percent for dogs**, driven by a much higher rate of customer return and higher dog ownership per customer than expected. Many annual and founding members are visiting Skiptown between five to seven days a week!*

No doubt, these results are remarkable, but here's what stuck out to me: Meggie had a prediction for how every single one of these things would go before they happened. She had gone through the levers process several times over the years and was able to build a financial model so dialed in that she had a mathematical prediction for how every activity in the business would play out: when dogs would show up, how many beers a pet owner would have while at the bar, how much ice she would melt through, and how many hours the person shaking that ice would work—all captured in rows in a spreadsheet, each based on real data.

Meggie knew her levers.

## BRINGING EVERYTHING TOGETHER

So far in this book, we have talked about deeply understanding your customers and what drives them to make decisions to purchase your product or service. We spent time figuring out your revenue formula. Then we had to decide how to prioritize all of the competing demands on your company and your time to build a roadmap to prioritize your actions. In the last chapter, we discussed KPIs and measuring how you are doing.

These are the four pillars of company success, but you can do each of them perfectly and still not have success. You see, it all has to come together as one cohesive model, and *you* as the leader of the company must understand what is necessary to make the business successful and what levers you should be pulling on to have the greatest impact or likelihood of success.

You see, without customers, you cannot have a real business. Figuring out your W3 is critical to making sure you truly understand them and their motivations. It is not enough to have customers if you cannot generate revenue from them, so a deep understanding of the drivers of your revenue formula is the next step. Now you know that you can generate revenue. Of course, you have to prioritize the use of your two scarce resources—time and money—and you need KPIs to track progress.

But how much capital will it take to become cash flow positive? How long will it take? What are the tradeoffs that you can make? How do you create more value for yourself and the other founders—by bootstrapping or raising capital? If raising, how much should you raise and when? Life would be so much easier if you had a crystal ball.

When my co-founders and I first started SurePayroll in 1999, it was the first internet payroll company in the country. We wanted to know the answers to the questions in this chapter but had no idea how to figure them out. Then we built a very detailed, bottom-up financial model. This was not a static document but rather a dynamic tool that we constantly updated, and as we learned more (mostly through running tests), we were able to modify the model further and further. Within a few months, it actually felt like we had a crystal ball. Predicting next month's customer count, revenue, and expenses was getting easier and easier. Looking out six to twelve months, the model was still pretty on target. The further we looked out, the less accurate it was at predicting the actual numbers, but as time went on and we had more months of actualized metrics, we could see the impact those metrics would have in the future.

For example, when we started, we assumed our customers would average the same headcount as the customers of Paychex (a competitor)—fourteen employees. This was a critical number for us since we generated revenue based on the number of paychecks we cut each pay period. It turned out that we skewed smaller than Paychex with 6.5 employees per company. Once we knew this, we could input 6.5 as the average number of employees per company and *see* the impact it would have on our future. It really was like having a crystal ball.

## WHAT IS A FINANCIAL MODEL?

There are lots of tools for managing your business:

- **Traditional Accounting Statements** (income statement, balance sheet, statement of cash flow)—They are great at formalizing what happened in the past—the past month, past quarter, or past year. The analogy to driving a car would be that these are like looking in the rearview mirror at what happened in the past.
- **KPIs**—They are great for telling you what is going on in your business right now. It is critical to know what is happening now, but continuing the car analogy, KPIs are like the dashboard of your car—speed, RPMs, oil pressure, and so on.
- **Financial Model**—This is the only way to look up the road and know what is going to happen in the future. It is like looking out the windshield at the road ahead. Just as it is almost impossible to successfully drive without being able to see the road in front of you, it is equally difficult to run a successful business without a good financial model.

So how is this "financial model" so different? Isn't it just a set of projections? What is the big deal?

The financial model is the *full mathematical representation* of how your business works, all the drivers and how they interact. It has *inputs* such as the amount of capital raised, the number of salespeople you have, what percentage of your customers churn each month, and more—these are represented as assumptions. It also has outputs, and the *output* of the financial model is a set of financial projections, including the three standard financial statements: an income statement, balance sheet, and a statement of cash flows.[6]

You see, the same model can produce very different projections with different inputs. If you change the number of salespeople you have, that cascades and impacts almost everything: sales, salaries and commissions, support costs, rent, and so forth. Changing that one input will potentially have a *huge* impact on your future and will be seen in the output from the model—the financial projections.

If you think about the first four chapters of this book, they were about understanding the drivers of your business and what matters. Now we are going to quantify those drivers in a spreadsheet to show what impact each has and give you a crystal ball into the future of your business.

When done well, it takes all the guessing out of operating a business—you know what the drivers are, and you run experiments to find out the data you need to be able to accurately predict your future.

## WHY SHOULD YOU BUILD A FINANCIAL MODEL?

Before we get started, we should have a clear objective—as a business builder, if you do not have a clear reason for doing

---

6   Although a financial model utilizes the three standard financial statements as its primary output, we don't go into depth about their mechanics in this chapter. For a very accessible introduction to basic accounting principles, see *The Accounting Game* by Darrell Mullis and Judith Orloff.

something, you should not waste time on it. Everything has to have a purpose. I actually have two purposes for building a financial model:

1. It will help you run your business better, allowing you to see the impact that today's decisions will have on your results tomorrow.
2. It will help you raise money more easily, should you choose to (or need to).

If you want to run your business better or make raising capital easier, then buckle up for the ride. If neither of those objectives is interesting to you, then you're probably not going to find this book useful.

## RUN YOUR BUSINESS BETTER

If you have a well-thought-out model, you should be able to ask questions such as, "If I raise prices by 10 percent, how much additional churn am I willing to accept and still be ahead of the game?" or "If I double down on advertising and spend twice as much each month on paid ads, will that help or hurt my cash flow?"

These are questions that can help you make important business decisions and take the guesswork out of being a CEO.

It is almost like having a virtual reality version of your business that you can "test drive" and try as many different permutations as you want and see what happens with each one. You can understand the impact of decisions without having to waste time and money to find out. It is like having that crystal ball.

## RAISE CAPITAL

Although most founders think of venture capitalists as huge risk takers, the good ones are great at mitigating risk in an inherently risky environment. One of the best ways to help the investor feel less risk is to walk them through a financial model that you have built—complete with the assumptions that you can tweak to play what-if with the investor.

When I was raising capital for SurePayroll, I got each investor who expressed serious interest to sit down with me and one of their analysts for ninety minutes to walk through the model. Each of the investors who did that with me either invested in the company or offered to invest in the company and we turned them down—100 percent.

Walking through the model gave them two things: a deep understanding of how the business works and what drivers were critical to its success, and confidence in me as an operator that I really understood the business and would figure it out. I think the financial model was the single most powerful tool we had when raising capital.

## WHO BUILDS THE MODEL?

Now that you see why a financial model is so valuable, what does it take to build one? I strongly believe that it should be *built by a founder or CEO* from the bottom up so that it incorporates all the nuances of your business.

There are some templates you can find on the web, and there are even some software packages that promise to ask a few questions and then generate a financial model for you, but I have yet to see one that is satisfactory. Most are much too simple, treating all businesses the same. But all software as a service (SaaS) businesses—or consumer, manufacturing, or retail businesses—do not work the same way—from sales cycles to contract length, to churn, to sales compensation, there are so many differences!

Most tools I have seen are too simple to capture these subtleties, and even if there were one that was capable of capturing all the details, it would have hundreds of parameters and be too difficult to use. A spreadsheet has the advantage of having only the details that you need, yet being able to have almost any nuance you want to incorporate.

There is learning and a level of understanding about the nuances of your business that come from struggling to take what you know in your head and create a mathematical formula for it. In fact, all of the authors in this book *unanimously* agree on this point. *You* need to build the model yourself early on, and as your business matures, even if there is a team member in finance responsible for it, you will sit side-by-side with them to help evolve it.

There are no shortcuts here. Although you can definitely *learn* from looking at other people's models as examples and to make sure you haven't missed important sections, it's up to *you to build your own from scratch.* I have tried taking a model that I previously built and rewire it. At first, I was so proud of myself that I could save a lot of time, but in the end, I encountered more and more issues, put more and more duct tape on the model, and ultimately had to trash it and start over.

For the engineers out there, it would be like getting the source code to a different business and just start tweaking it to fit yours. Maybe you get something that limps along for a while, but you always end up having to rewrite it as the technical debt gets bigger and bigger. Do yourself a favor and do this one right the first time!

## GETTING STARTED

I have made up a fictitious company that is crafted to show many of the dimensions of a modern internet company from how it gets its customers to how it makes money. I have called it Dollar Cave Club with the tongue-in-cheek tagline, "Everything you need to make your man cave." It's my poor attempt at poking fun of the brogrammer startup culture, but it'll serve our purposes. Here's a description:

> Dollar Cave Club is the latest in a series of companies that make recurring purchases easy and painless. Sign up for our $29.99 monthly subscription, and we will send you a box each month with essentials for your man cave. One month, it is a classic poker set, the next an amazing set of beer steins. If you cannot wait to get your favorite dartboard, you can come to the site directly and buy anything we sell.

> We get most of our new customers from search engine optimization (SEO), advertising on Google and Facebook. We have such a highly desirable audience that many people want to advertise to our visitors on our site as well.

> Subscribers can add on to their monthly subscription by selecting any items in our catalog, and shipping is free! Our churn has been around 4 percent per month. The traffic to our site is growing nicely, as are our sales.

Before you can build a financial model for a company, you need to understand how it really works and what drives it. You can use Chapters 1–4 of this book to think critically about Dollar Cave Club and its W3, revenue formula, KPIs, and roadmap. Understanding each of these will be critical to building the financial model.

Over the rest of the chapter, I will take you step by step through how to build a financial model from scratch, using the Dollar Cave Club as the example. To make following along easier, we've created the full version of the financial model for you to download and play with as we go.

Download a copy of Dollar Cave Club's financial model at leversbook.com/DollarCaveClubModel.

## START WITH THE ASSUMPTIONS

Building a complete financial model feels like a daunting task, and just like other daunting tasks, I like to start by writing down everything I know. In the financial model, we start with the first tab of the spreadsheet's workbook, labeling it "Assumptions," and create all the variables we easily know. Reviewing the description I laid out earlier, here are some of the things we know about Dollar Cave Club:

- The monthly subscription price is $29.99.
- The monthly churn rate of subscribers is 4 percent.
- We get customers through SEO, search engine marketing (SEM), and Facebook.
- We also have add-on revenue and advertising revenue.

Each of these knowns become assumptions in our spreadsheet.

Eventually, we'll have a whole host of assumptions for both revenue and expenses spelled out in the "Assumptions" tab that the rest of the model will use to create our outputs, as you can see in figure 5.1.

## Dollar Shave Club

ASSUMPTIONS

| | |
|---|---:|
| Subscription Price | $29.99 |
| Churn on subscriptions per month | 4% |
| | |
| Page views per visit | 3.5 |
| CPM growth per month on ads sold | 10% |
| Max CPM on ads sold | $1.50 |
| | |
| Steady State Monthly SEM Spend | $10,000 |
| Steady State Monthly FB spend | $10,000 |
| Maximum marketing spend of Cash Balance | |
| | |
| SEM -> Subscription Conversion | 2.00% |
| Facebook -> Subscriber Conversion | 1.00% |
| | |
| SEM -> eCommerce Conversion | 4.50% |
| Facebook -> eCommerce Conversion | 2.50% |
| | |
| Organic Traffic -> Subscriber Conversion | 0.20% |
| Organic Traffic -> eCommerce Conversion | 0.50% |
| | |
| Organic SEO Traffic monthly growth rate | 10% |
| Direct Traffic Multiplier | 33% |
| | |
| Average CPC on SEM (Google) | $2.25 |
| Average CPC on Facebook | $1.85 |
| Visits per FB Post with Picture | 5 |
| Visits per FB Post with Video | 25 |
| | |
| Subscription Margin | 25.00% |
| eCommerce Margin | 30.00% |
| | |
| Internet Infrastructure base cost / mo | $500.0 |
| Incremental for each 1 million visits | $250.0 |
| | |
| Orders / warehouse help person | 5000 |
| | |
| Taxes and benefits load | 25% |
| Rent per employee per month | $500.0 |
| Tech Cost per employee per month | $100.0 |
| Legal and Accounting Cost per month | $500.0 |
| | |
| Travel cost per employee per month | $250.0 |
| Training Buidget per employee per month | $100.0 |
| Recruiting per added employee | $5,000.0 |
| | |
| Opening Cash Balance | $1,000,000.0 |
| Raise at Month 13 | $2,500,000.0 |
| | |
| Average Accounts Receivable Days | 30 |
| Average Accounts Payable Days | 60 |
| Inventory Days On Hand | 30 |

**Figure 5.1**

If this list starts to overwhelm you, don't worry. You don't need to have this many assumptions in your model when you start. Just start with all the things you easily know about this business now. As you build out your model, you'll uncover new assumptions you'll need to make and add them as you go.

Notice also in the model that I use color and shaded cells for assumptions to make it easy for the reader to know what was typed in and what was not. **Every cell that is not an assumption (no shading) is a formula.** There are no typed numbers in those cells, just formulas.

With the exception of your labels or historical data, if you are thinking about typing a number in *anywhere*, it should be an assumption.

## LAY OUT THE INCOME STATEMENT

Next, we can create the three standard financial statements as an output of the model: the income statement, balance sheet, and statement of cash flows. Create those three tabs, each labeled as the "Monthly" version because when we are almost finished, we will roll up the monthly numbers to create annual versions of each as well.

In your monthly income statement, type in the categories of the income statement as rows in the left-most column:

- Revenue
- Cost of Goods Sold (COGS) or Direct Expenses
- Gross Profit
- Indirect Expenses
- Net Profit

If you're not familiar with the structure of an income statement, we'll cover each category in more detail later in the chapter. For now, we're just going to focus on that top row: revenue, or the money that your business is bringing in.

## MONTHLY INCOME STATEMENT

**Dollar Shave Club** ⊗

**Revenue**
Subscription
Add-ons
eCommerce
Advertising
**Total Sales**

Internet
Subscription
eCommerce
**Total Direct Costs**
**Gross Profit**
Digital Marketing Spend
**Contribution Margin**
Indirect Costs (Salaries, Rent, etc.)
**EBITDA**
Employees
Capital Raised
Cash Burn
Capital Reserve

Figure 5.2

Pro Tip: As you create the rest of your tabs, you can use the monthly income statement as the one place you type in your column headers ("Jan-20," "Feb-20," etc.). Then you can reference those column headers (i.e., ='Monthly Income Statement'!C2) in the rest of your monthly tabs rather than retyping them all each time. You can do the same with the row headers for the annual income statement. This will make maintaining the model much easier.

## FIGURE OUT WHERE REVENUE COMES FROM

Now that we have some structure, we need to dive in and figure out what number (or numbers) to input for revenue for the first month of the model.

Where do we get the revenue figures? Remember, this is a *model*, so it should change as assumptions change. So instead of typing numbers into the spreadsheet, each cell needs to be a formula—your revenue formula. (I told you that all those previous chapters of work would be valuable here.)

## USING HISTORICAL DATA IN YOUR MODEL

If you can, you should have at least a year's worth of *actual* numbers on your financial model's income statement that are hard-coded numbers from your actual historical performance. Shade them a different color to make it obvious that they represent something different. It will make it easier for the reader to understand your business and should help you calibrate the model as well.

For Dollar Cave Club, we will start with the primary revenue, which is subscription revenue. At its most basic level, the revenue formula for subscriptions is:

Number of Subscribers × Subscription Price

The subscription price is an assumption we got from the description and something that we'll treat as constant throughout the model, so we can just reference that from the "Assumptions" tab.

Here's the challenging part: how do we figure out how many

subscribers we have at any given time? In other words, what drives the number of subscribers?

This is where we are going to spend most of our time: understanding the levers we have that are going to get us more subscribers and then figure out how to build those into the model.

## FIGURE OUT WHERE SUBSCRIBERS COME FROM

Since there's still a lot of work, I need to figure out what our revenue will be each month. I create a new tab titled Revenue Drivers. In that tab, I list the core drivers that make up how many subscribers I'll have at the end of each month: the number of subscribers I had last month, the number of new subscribers I got this month, and the number of subscribers I lost this month.

Beginning (or Last Month's) Subscribers + New Subscribers – Lost (Churned) Subscribers = Ending Subscribers

## Dollar Shave Club ⊗

| Revenue | Jan-20 | Feb-20 | Mar-20 | Apr-20 | May-20 | Jun-20 | Jul-20 | Jul-20 | Aug-20 | Sep-20 | Oct-20 | Nov-20 | Dec-20 | 2020 |
|---|---|---|---|---|---|---|---|---|---|---|---|---|---|---|
| Beginning Subscribers | 100 | 102 | 105 | 112 | 119 | 268 | 411 | 550 | 683 | 812 | 937 | 1,057 | 1,173 | |
| New Subscribers | 6 | 7 | 11 | 11 | 154 | 154 | 155 | 155 | 156 | 157 | 157 | 158 | 159 | 1,440 |
| Churn Percentage | 4% | 4% | 4% | 4% | 4% | 4% | 4% | 4% | 4% | 4% | 4% | 4% | 4% | 4% |
| Lost Subscribers | 4 | 4 | 4 | 4 | 5 | 11 | 16 | 22 | 27 | 32 | 37 | 42 | 47 | 255 |
| Ending Subscribers | 102 | 105 | 112 | 119 | 268 | 411 | 550 | 683 | 812 | 937 | 1,057 | 1,173 | 1,285 | 1,285 |
| Average Subscription | $29.99 | $29.99 | $29.99 | $29.99 | $29.99 | $29.99 | $29.99 | $29.99 | $29.99 | $29.99 | $29.99 | $29.99 | $29.99 | $29.99 |
| **Subscription Revenue** | **$3,059** | **$3,149** | **$3,359** | **$3,569** | **$8,037** | **$12,326** | **$16,495** | **$20,483** | **$24,352** | **$28,101** | **$31,699** | **$35,178** | **$38,537** | **$228,344** |
| % of Add Ons | 10.00% | 10.50% | 11.00% | 11.50% | 12.00% | 12.50% | 13.00% | 13.50% | 14.00% | 14.50% | 15.00% | 15.50% | 16.00% | 16.00% |
| Average Add On | 22 | 22 | 22 | 22 | 22 | 22 | 22 | 22 | 22 | 22 | 22 | 22 | 22 | 22 |
| **Add On Revenue** | **$229** | **$248** | **$277** | **$308** | **$723** | **$1,156** | **$1,608** | **$2,074** | **$2,557** | **$3,056** | **$3,566** | **$4,089** | **$4,624** | **$24,516** |
| eCommerce orders | 14 | 17 | 26 | 27 | 362 | 363 | 365 | 366 | 367 | 369 | 371 | 373 | 375 | |
| Average Order Size | $35 | $36 | $36 | $37 | $38 | $39 | $39 | $40 | $41 | $42 | $43 | $44 | $44 | $44 |
| **eCommerce Revenue** | **$490** | **$607** | **$947** | **$1,003** | **$13,714** | **$14,027** | **$14,387** | **$14,715** | **$15,050** | **$15,435** | **$15,829** | **$16,232** | **$16,646** | **$139,081** |
| Page Views | 5,108 | 6,847 | 8,508 | 9,080 | 53,266 | 54,120 | 55,034 | 56,020 | 57,080 | 58,227 | 59,469 | 60,815 | 62,277 | |
| Ad impressions per page | 1 | 1 | 1 | 1 | 1 | 1 | 1 | 1 | 1 | 1 | 2 | 2 | 2 | 2 |
| Average CPM | 1 | 1 | 1 | 1 | 1 | 1 | 1 | 1 | 1 | 1 | 1 | 1 | 1 | 2 |
| **Advertising Revenue** | **$1** | **$2** | **$4** | **$5** | **$35** | **$44** | **$54** | **$65** | **$80** | **$96** | **$116** | **$139** | **$159** | **$799** |
| **Total Revenue** | **$3,780** | **$4,006** | **$4,586** | **$4,884** | **$22,510** | **$27,552** | **$32,543** | **$37,337** | **$42,038** | **$46,687** | **$51,210** | **$55,639** | **$59,966** | **$392,740** |

Figure 5.3

Here's how we can calculate each one:

- **Beginning Subscribers:** With the Dollar Cave Club model, we've already added historical data, so the last month's subscribers are already in your spreadsheet, so that part is easy.
- **Lost Subscribers:** We can calculate churned subscribers by multiplying last month's subscribers with the monthly churn rate (which we have as an assumption in the "Assumptions" tab).
- **New Subscribers:** The number of new subscribers for this month is harder to predict. But we do know that to get any new subscribers, they have to show up on our website first. So new subscribers are a function of (1) the number of visits (or web traffic) we get and (2) how many of those visits we can convert to purchase a monthly subscription.

So the next step is to figure out where those visits come from.

## FIGURE OUT WHERE VISITS COME FROM

Here are the drivers for visits with the Dollar Cave Club:

- **Spend on Google Ads**—that directly leads to visits from Google users.
- **Spend on Facebook Ads**—that directly leads to visits from Facebook users.
- **Facebook Picture Posts**—that predictably leads to a certain number of curious users visiting our site.
- **Facebook Video Posts**—that also predictably leads to a certain number of curious users visiting our site, and since there is higher engagement with video, that leads to more visits per post than pictures.
- **Direct Traffic**—people who type in "www.DollarCaveClub.

com," who already know of the brand and want to look or hopefully buy. Although this is very hard to control, over time, it does become easier to predict when you are tracking your metrics diligently.

- **Search Traffic (SEO)**—people who are searching for something on the web and land on our site. We can indirectly control this by doing a lot of SEO, but it's still difficult to control.

To account for each of these drivers, I create another tab in the workbook labeled Web Traffic Drivers.

When it's done, it will look like this:

TRAFFIC DETAIL

# Dollar Shave Club ✦

| Revenue | Jan-20 | Feb-20 | Mar-20 | Apr-20 | May-20 | Jun-20 | Jul-20 | Jul-20 | Aug-20 | Sep-20 | Oct-20 | Nov-20 | Dec-20 | 2020 |
|---|---|---|---|---|---|---|---|---|---|---|---|---|---|---|
| Monthly CPC Spend | 250 | 250 | 500 | 500 | 10,000 | 10,000 | 10,000 | 10,000 | 10,000 | 10,000 | 10,000 | 10,000 | 10,000 | |
| SEM (Google) | 111 | 111 | 222 | 222 | 4,444 | 4,444 | 4,444 | 4,444 | 4,444 | 4,444 | 4,444 | 4,444 | 4,444 | 40,667 |
| Monthly Facebook Spend | 250 | 250 | 500 | 500 | 10,000 | 10,000 | 10,000 | 10,000 | 10,000 | 10,000 | 10,000 | 10,000 | 10,000 | |
| Traffic from FACEBOOK | 135 | 135 | 270 | 270 | 5,405 | 5,405 | 5,405 | 5,405 | 5,405 | 5,405 | 5,405 | 5,405 | 5,405 | 49,459 |
| Facebook Picture Posts | 20 | 20 | 20 | 20 | 20 | 20 | 20 | 20 | 20 | 20 | 20 | 20 | 20 | |
| Facebook traffic (Pictures) | 100 | 100 | 100 | 100 | 100 | 100 | 100 | 100 | 100 | 100 | 100 | 100 | 100 | |
| Facebook Video Posts | 12 | 12 | 12 | 12 | 12 | 12 | 12 | 12 | 12 | 12 | 12 | 12 | 12 | |
| Facebook traffic (Video) | 300 | 300 | 300 | 300 | 300 | 300 | 300 | 300 | 300 | 300 | 300 | 300 | 300 | |
| Direct Traffic | 213 | 610 | 728 | 771 | 3,905 | 4,002 | 4,103 | 4,207 | 4,315 | 4,429 | 4,548 | 4,673 | 4,805 | 41,309 |
| SEO visits | 1,000 | 1,100 | 1,210 | 1,331 | 1,464 | 1,611 | 1,772 | 1,949 | 2,144 | 2,358 | 2,594 | 2,853 | 3,138 | 24,523 |
| **Total Visits** | **1,460** | **1,956** | **2,431** | **2,594** | **15,219** | **15,463** | **15,724** | **16,006** | **16,309** | **16,636** | **16,991** | **17,376** | **17,794** | **155,958** |

Figure 5.4

Looking at these different drivers of visits (we can call them subdrivers), we see that the first four are easy to control directly. If we spend more money on advertising through Google or Facebook, we'll get more visits. Likewise, if we post more videos or pictures, we will get more visits. That means we can set assumptions to calculate the number of actual visits from each subdriver.

We can use spend on Google ads as an example. Here's what I know about spending on Google ads:

- Google charges me for every person who clicks on my ad and visits my site. This is the Cost per Click (CPC).
- I can divide the amount of money I spend on ads by the CPC to calculate the number of visits to my site from Google ads.

Since CPC isn't going to fluctuate every month, I add that to my "Assumptions" tab. Because I may choose to ratchet my spending up or down month to month, I also create a row in the "Web Traffic Driver" tab for monthly CPC spend so that I can change a month if I choose (see figure 5.4).

Then I can do the same for Facebook ads: I add the price Facebook charges me for a click as an assumption in the "Assumptions" tab, and then I add the amount of money I spend on Facebook ads as assumptions for each month in "Web Traffic Drivers."

Facebook video and picture posts work similarly, but instead of setting assumptions around my spend and the CPC, I can make assumptions around how many posts I make each month and how many visits each post will generate.

SEO and direct visits are much harder to directly control, but I can still make some assumptions around how they grow. For direct visits, it turns out that the more visits from ads and social media, the more direct visits you get, so I can make the number of direct visits to the site a function of the total other visits. To do that, I add a multiplier of 0.33 in the "Assumptions" tab. In other words, I assume I will get thirty-three direct visits for every hundred other visits.

For simplicity's sake, I assume a monthly growth rate of SEO traffic of 10 percent and add that to the "Assumptions" tab. Eventually, I might decide to break down the SEO drivers, and when I do, I can incorporate them into the model. I've summarized the formulas we just created in the following table.

| WEB TRAFFIC DRIVER | FORMULA |
| --- | --- |
| Visits from SEM (Google) | = Google Ad Spend per Month/CPC on Google |
| Visits from Facebook Ads | = Facebook Ad Spend per Month/CPC on Facebook |
| Visits from Facebook Picture Posts | = Facebook Picture Posts per Month × Visits per Facebook Picture Post |
| Visits from Facebook Video Posts | = Facebook Video Posts per Month × Visits per Facebook Video Post |
| Visits from Direct Visits | = Total Other Visits × Direct Traffic Multiplier |
| Visits from SEO | = Last Month's SEO Visits × Organic SEO Traffic Monthly Growth Rate |

Now that we have the web traffic drivers, we can calculate the number of web visits in any month based on the spend in advertising and hard work in creating social media posts.

This is a critical point to understand: I am *not* just hoping that web traffic will grow by some impressive percentage each month but rather breaking down the traffic into its components and then looking at what levers I can use to impact each of them. In this case, growth is primarily driven by advertising spend, social medial posts, and SEO.

These are the levers that you have to drive growth. If you do not understand the levers, you cannot effectively grow your business.

## MOVING FROM VISITS BACK TO SUBSCRIBERS

Now we must do the hard work of calculating how traffic converts into revenue. To do that, we go back up one level to the "Revenue Drivers" tab.

Remember that all that work we did identifying our web traffic drivers was to help us predict how many new subscribers we get each month. Now we can go back to that new subscriber row and create our formula. To do so, we need two things:

- The amount of traffic from each source
- Our assumed conversion rate for each of those sources

Facebook clicks convert differently than Google clicks, which convert differently than organic traffic (which can come through SEO, direct, or our Facebook picture or video posts). Once you know the traffic you are getting from each source, you can multiply it by the conversion rate for that source and compute the number of new subscribers for that month. In this model, we set three assumptions for the different visits to subscriber conversion rates:

- A conversion rate from web traffic from our Facebook ads: 1 percent
- A conversion rate from web traffic from Google ads (SEM): 2 percent
- A conversion rate from organic web traffic: 0.2 percent

You now have everything you need to model the number of subscribers for *any* month:

Traffic × Conversion Rate = Subscribers

Once you know the number of subscribers, you can apply the revenue formula to get the revenue from subscriptions.

Subscribers × Subscription Price = Revenue

## FACTORING IN ADDITIONAL REVENUE

In this business, subscriptions drive most of the revenue and even the secondary revenue. There is a second revenue formula for add-on revenue, and it is just a function of what percentage of the subscribers add on to their monthly subscription and how much they add on. (Again, these are assumptions to be validated.)

There is a third revenue formula for e-commerce orders, also driven by the web traffic but using different conversion rates than we used for conversion to subscriptions. Since e-commerce orders are generally not recurring revenue, you do not need to track last month's orders and so forth. Instead, just multiply the traffic from a particular source (SEM, social, SEO, direct) by the appropriate conversion assumption to get the e-commerce revenue for that month.

In this model, we also have a fourth revenue formula that comes from selling advertising space on our site. It is:

Visits × Average Page Views per Visit × Impressions per Page × Revenue per Impression

It, too, is driven by traffic to the site, which means I can just use the total traffic to the site and not worry about different sources—for advertising purposes, a page view is a page view.

Now, on the "Revenue Drivers" tab, we have all four types of revenue calculated for every month of the model (I generally go out five years). We can then go back to the monthly income statement, list the four kinds of revenue, and pull the dollar values from the "Revenue Drivers" tab.

MONTHLY INCOME STATEMENT
**Dollar Shave Club**

| Revenue | Jan-20 | Feb-20 | Mar-20 | Apr-20 | May-20 | Jun-20 | Jul-20 | Jul-20 | Aug-20 | Sep-20 | Oct-20 | Nov-20 | Dec-20 | 2020 |
|---|---|---|---|---|---|---|---|---|---|---|---|---|---|---|
| Subscription | 3,059 | 3,149 | 3,359 | 3,569 | 8,037 | 12,326 | 16,495 | 20,483 | 24,352 | 28,101 | 31,699 | 35,178 | 38,537 | 228,344 |
| Add-ons | 229 | 248 | 277 | 308 | 723 | 1,156 | 1,808 | 2,074 | 2,557 | 3,056 | 3,566 | 4,089 | 4,624 | 24,516 |
| eCommerce | 490 | 607 | 947 | 1,003 | 13,714 | 14,027 | 14,387 | 14,715 | 15,050 | 15,435 | 15,829 | 16,232 | 16,646 | 139,081 |
| Advertising | 1 | 2 | 4 | 5 | 35 | 44 | 54 | 65 | 80 | 96 | 116 | 139 | 159 | 799 |
| **Total Sales** | 3,780 | 4,006 | 4,586 | 4,884 | 22,510 | 27,552 | 32,543 | 37,337 | 42,038 | 46,687 | 51,210 | 55,639 | 59,966 | 392,740 |

Figure 5.5

If you're following along, you have just completed the most important and most difficult part of building a model: figuring out where your revenue comes from and what drivers there are. From here, it gets much easier.

## CALCULATING EXPENSES

Of course, revenue is the *most important* part of the business and the most important part of the income statement if you want to be in control of your destiny. Effectively, 85–90 percent of your time and effort in modeling should be in figuring out what the revenue drivers are and predicting revenue. But without expenses, you do not have the full picture.

And all expenses are not created equal. I group expenses into three big buckets.

### Expense of delivering your product or service (Cost of Goods Sold [COGS])

These are expenses that grow linearly with revenue. If you are selling physical widgets, it is the cost of the widget, the packaging, the shipping cost, the labor to package and ship it. If you sold 2x the widgets, all those costs would go up by roughly 2x. If you sell software, the COGS is a much smaller percentage of the revenue but could include hosting fees, customer service people, training costs, and so forth. This is what determines your gross profit.

Revenue – COGS = Gross Profit

### Sales and marketing expenses

How much are you spending to get the next customers? This includes salespeople's salaries, marketing salaries, and all sales and marketing-related expenses, such as trade shows, customer dinners, Google ads, SEO, consulting, and so on.

### Indirect expenses

These are the expenses that are required to run the business but are not related to delivering the goods or services and not related to selling more. It could be the CEO's salary, rent, accounting and legal fees, and so forth. Many people call these fixed expenses, but I believe if you are an entrepreneur, you should never have the mindset that anything is a "fixed" expense. If the shit hits the fan and you need to cut costs, the CEO salary might be the first to go. You may have a five-year lease on office space, but if you need to, you will figure out how to cut that expense—by subleasing, renegotiating, or something else. I always prefer the term *indirect expenses* to remind myself that nothing is ever fixed in a startup.

Once I have bucketed the expenses this way, it allows me to format the income statement so that I better understand how the business is doing and when I can expect it to get to profitability.

When talking about one transaction, revenue, COGS is called contribution margin. However, when you roll it up for the entire company and possibly add in some things that are difficult to allocate on a transaction-by-transaction basis such as customer service or warehouse labor, then it is called gross profit.

Gross profit gives me an idea of how much I need to grow revenue to cover all the other expenses. For example, if gross profit is $50K/month and my other expenses are $150K/month, then I need 3x the revenue to break even.

After gross profit, I like to see all the sales and marketing expenses. That gives me an idea of what it costs me to get more revenue. This is looked at very differently if it is a recurring revenue business such as SaaS rather than each sale needing to be sold each time as in a car dealership. In either example, it is critical to understand how much you are spending to get new revenue. Of course, it should be less than the lifetime value (LTV) of the revenue, as measured not in revenue but in contribution margin.

I see so many entrepreneurs calculate lifetime revenue and call it LTV, but that is just another case of not being intellectually honest with yourself. You have costs associated with delivering that revenue, and you had better understand them and account for them.

The next section of the income statement is the indirect costs. Although there are a lot of indirect costs in a business and many entrepreneurs just accept them, good entrepreneurs try to minimize them, as they are not related to delivering revenue or getting revenue. They are just drag on your income statement.

A well-formatted income statement for Dollar Cave Club is depicted in figure 5.6.

Figure 5.6

MONTHLY INCOME STATEMENT

## Dollar Shave Club ⊗

| Revenue | Jan-20 | Feb-20 | Mar-20 | Apr-20 | May-20 | Jun-20 | Jul-20 | Jul-20 | Aug-20 | Sep-20 | Oct-20 | Nov-20 | Dec-20 | 2020 |
|---|---|---|---|---|---|---|---|---|---|---|---|---|---|---|
| Subscription | $3,059 | $3,149 | $3,359 | $3,569 | $8,037 | $12,326 | $16,495 | $20,483 | $24,352 | $28,101 | $31,699 | $35,178 | $38,537 | $228,344 |
| Add-ons | 229 | 248 | 277 | 308 | 723 | 1,156 | 1,608 | 2,074 | 2,557 | 3,056 | 3,566 | 4,089 | 4,624 | 24,516 |
| eCommerce | 490 | 607 | 947 | 1,003 | 13,714 | 14,027 | 14,387 | 14,715 | 15,050 | 15,435 | 15,829 | 16,232 | 16,646 | 139,081 |
| Advertising | 1 | 2 | 4 | 5 | 35 | 44 | 54 | 65 | 80 | 96 | 116 | 139 | 159 | 799 |
| **Total Sales** | **3,780** | **4,006** | **4,586** | **4,884** | **22,510** | **27,552** | **32,543** | **37,337** | **42,038** | **46,687** | **51,210** | **55,639** | **59,966** | **392,740** |
| | | | | | | | | | | | | | | |
| Internet | 500 | 500 | 501 | 501 | 504 | 504 | 504 | 504 | 504 | 504 | 504 | 504 | 504 | 6,539 |
| Subscription | 2,294 | 2,362 | 2,519 | 2,677 | 6,028 | 9,244 | 12,371 | 15,362 | 18,264 | 21,075 | 23,775 | 26,384 | 28,903 | 171,258 |
| eCommerce | 343 | 425 | 663 | 702 | 9,600 | 9,819 | 10,071 | 10,300 | 10,535 | 10,804 | 11,080 | 11,363 | 11,652 | 97,357 |
| **Total Direct Costs** | **3,138** | **3,287** | **3,683** | **3,879** | **16,132** | **19,567** | **22,946** | **26,167** | **29,303** | **32,384** | **35,359** | **38,251** | **41,059** | **275,153** |
| **Gross Profit** | **642** | **719** | **904** | **1,005** | **6,378** | **7,985** | **9,598** | **11,171** | **12,735** | **14,303** | **15,851** | **17,388** | **18,907** | **117,586** |
| Digital Marketing Spend | 500 | 500 | 1,000 | 1,000 | 20,000 | 20,000 | 20,000 | 20,000 | 20,000 | 20,000 | 20,000 | 20,000 | 20,000 | 20,000 |
| **Contribution Margin** | **142** | **219** | **(96)** | **5** | **(13,622)** | **(12,015)** | **(10,402)** | **(8,829)** | **(7,265)** | **(5,697)** | **(4,149)** | **(2,612)** | **(1,093)** | **97,586** |
| Indirect Costs (Salaries, Rent, etc.) | 39,717 | 39,717 | 67,242 | 73,608 | 68,608 | 68,608 | 68,608 | 68,608 | 68,608 | 68,608 | 68,608 | 68,608 | 84,975 | 79,975 |
| **EBITDA** | **(39,575)** | **(39,498)** | **(67,338)** | **(73,603)** | **(82,230)** | **(80,623)** | **(79,011)** | **(77,438)** | **(75,873)** | **(74,305)** | **(72,757)** | **(71,220)** | **(86,068)** | **17,611** |
| Employees | 4 | 4 | 6 | 7 | 7 | 7 | 7 | 7 | 7 | 7 | 7 | 7 | 8 | 8 |
| Capital Raised | $1,000,000 | | | | | | | | | | | | | |
| Cash Burn | (39,575) | (39,498) | (67,338) | (73,603) | (82,230) | (80,623) | (79,011) | (77,438) | (75,873) | (74,305) | (72,757) | (71,220) | (86,068) | (919,539) |
| Capital Reserve | $960,425 | $920,928 | $853,590 | $779,987 | $697,757 | $617,133 | $538,123 | $460,685 | $384,812 | $310,507 | $237,750 | $166,530 | $80,461 | $80,461 |

Building the formulas for the expenses should be straightforward. All the COGS-related expenses will be directly related to the revenue numbers that you have already calculated (since these are direct expenses that grow with every new product you sell). The sales and marketing-related expenses drive the revenue, so you should have already built them out as revenue drivers when building the revenue section. In our case, these expenses are CPC and Facebook spend. The indirect expenses are all relatively simple and do not vary much by definition.

Once you have a monthly income statement that you are comfortable with, you can roll it up into an annual income statement by creating a new tab, referencing all the row labels from the monthly income statement (so they match exactly even if you change a label), and then creating a column for each year where the cells in that column are a sum of the twelve months of cells in the corresponding row of the monthly income statement.

## Dollar Shave Club ✗

| | 2020 | 2021 | 2022 | 2023 | 2024 |
|---|---|---|---|---|---|
| **Revenue** | | | | | |
| Subscription | 190,347 | 655,611 | 1,021,729 | 1,447,707 | 2,339,520 |
| Add-ons | 19,788 | 92,169 | 153,259 | 217,156 | 350,928 |
| eCommerce | 121,332 | 231,228 | 348,401 | 658,253 | 1,693,633 |
| Advertising | 599 | 2,425 | 4,195 | 9,489 | 26,052 |
| **Gross Revenue** | **$332,065** | **$981,434** | **$1,527,584** | **$2,332,605** | **$4,410,133** |
| **Direct Costs** | | | | | |
| Internet infrastructure | 6,035 | 6,062 | 6,105 | 6,238 | 6,653 |
| Subscription | 142,760 | 491,709 | 766,297 | 1,085,780 | 1,754,640 |
| eCommerce | 84,932 | 161,860 | 243,880 | 460,777 | 1,185,543 |
| **Total Costs** | **$233,727** | **$659,630** | **$1,016,283** | **$1,552,795** | **$2,946,836** |
| **Gross Profit** | **$98,338** | **$321,803** | **$511,302** | **$779,810** | **$1,463,297** |
| **Sales and Marketing Costs** | | | | | |
| CPC Spend | 81,206 | 120,000 | 120,000 | 120,000 | 120,000 |
| Facebook Spend | 81,499 | 120,000 | 120,000 | 120,000 | 120,000 |
| **Total Marketing Costs** | **$162,705** | **$240,000** | **$240,000** | **$240,000** | **$240,000** |
| **Gross Profit - Sales & Marketing** | **($64,367)** | **$81,803** | **$271,302** | **$539,810** | **$1,223,297** |
| **Indirect Costs** | | | | | |
| Salaries | 675,000 | 875,000 | 912,500 | 912,500 | 937,500 |
| Rent | 38,500 | 49,500 | 54,000 | 54,000 | 57,000 |
| Technology | 7,700 | 9,900 | 10,800 | 10,800 | 11,400 |
| Legal and Accounting | 6,000 | 6,000 | 6,000 | 6,000 | 6,000 |
| Travel | 19,250 | 24,750 | 27,000 | 27,000 | 28,500 |
| Training | 7,700 | 9,900 | 10,800 | 10,800 | 11,400 |
| Recruiting | 15,000 | 10,000 | - | - | 5,000 |
| **Total Indirect Costs** | **$769,150** | **$985,050** | **$1,021,100** | **$1,021,100** | **$1,056,800** |
| Employees | 7 | 9 | 9 | 9 | 10 |
| **EBITDA** | **($833,517)** | **($903,247)** | **($749,798)** | **($481,290)** | **$166,497** |

Figure 5.7: Image of Annual Income Statement

## BUILDING THE BALANCE SHEET AND STATEMENT OF CASH FLOW

The balance sheet and statement of cash flow can each be directly derived from the income statement with a light understanding of basic accounting principles. I personally don't care about the balance sheet (although it is the "language of the investor," so it will help) and more about the statement of cash flow, as that is what really matters in the early stages of the business. You can see Dollar Cave Club's balance sheet and statement of cash flow in figures 5.8 and 5.9.

BALANCE SHEET
**Dollar Shave Club** ⊗

| | 2020 | 2021 | 2022 | 2023 | 2024 |
|---|---|---|---|---|---|
| Assets: | | | | | |
| Cash | $159,383 | $1,737,182 | $967,606 | $449,442 | $508,210 |
| Accounts Receivable | 55,235 | 102,575 | 151,070 | 244,858 | 520,953 |
| Inventory | 41,426 | 76,931 | 113,303 | 183,643 | 390,715 |
| Fixed Assets | | | | | |
| Accumulated Depreciation | | | | | |
| **Total Assets** | **$256,043** | **$1,916,689** | **$1,231,979** | **$877,943** | **$1,419,877** |
| | | | | | |
| Liabilities | | | | | |
| Accounts Payable | 90,261 | 154,737 | 219,049 | 344,432 | 717,601 |
| Short Term Debt | | | | | |
| Long Term Debt | | | | | |
| **Total Liabilities** | **90,261** | **154,737** | **219,049** | **344,432** | **717,601** |
| | | | | | |
| Owners Equity | | | | | |
| Capital Stock | 1,000,000 | 3,500,000 | 3,500,000 | 3,500,000 | 3,500,000 |
| Retained Earnings | (834,218) | (1,738,049) | (2,487,070) | (2,966,489) | (2,797,724) |
| **Total Equity** | **165,782** | **1,761,951** | **1,012,930** | **533,511** | **702,276** |
| | | | | | |
| **Total Liabilities & Equity** | **$256,043** | **$1,916,689** | **$1,231,979** | **$877,943** | **$1,419,877** |

Figure 5.8

ANNUAL CASH FLOW
**Dollar Shave Club** ⊗

| | 2020 | 2021 | 2022 | 2023 | 2024 |
|---|---|---|---|---|---|
| Beginning Cash Balance | $0 | $157,693 | $1,736,200 | $965,995 | $446,027 |
| Cash Receipts: | | | | | |
| Gross Sales | 332,065 | 981,434 | 1,527,584 | 2,332,806 | 4,410,133 |
| Change in A/R | (55,503) | (47,038) | (48,149) | (93,651) | (276,026) |
| **Total Receipts** | **$276,562** | **$934,396** | **$1,479,435** | **$2,238,955** | **$4,134,107** |
| Disbursements: | | | | | |
| Gross Expenses | (1,165,582) | (1,984,680) | (2,277,383) | (2,813,895) | (4,243,636) |
| Change in A/P | 90,621 | 64,071 | 63,854 | 125,211 | 373,080 |
| Change in Inventory Value | (41,627) | (35,278) | (36,112) | (70,238) | (207,020) |
| Amortization & Depreciation | | | | | |
| Capital Expenditures | | | | | |
| Income Tax Paid | | | | | |
| **Total Disbursements** | **($1,116,587)** | **($1,855,888)** | **($2,249,640)** | **($2,758,922)** | **($4,077,576)** |
| Net Cash Flow from Operations | | | | | |
| Equity Financing | 1,000,000 | 2,500,000 | - | - | - |
| Interest Income | | | | | |
| **Ending Cash Balance** | **$157,693** | **$1,736,200** | **$965,995** | **$446,027** | **$502,558** |
| Lowest balance of the year | $157,693 | $1,736,200 | $965,995 | $446,027 | $368,482 |

Figure 5.9

If your business doesn't have a lot of working capital (inventory or payment terms with your customers and supplier), large fixed assets such as trucks and machinery, or large amounts of debt, there will be very little difference between the income statement and statement of cash flow. However, businesses that have significant accounts payable, account receivable, depreciation of capital equipment, and so forth need both the income statement and the statement of cash flow.

Once you have the model built, the magic starts to happen.

## PLAYING WHAT-IF SCENARIOS WITH THE FINANCIAL MODEL

Now that you have a mathematical representation of your business, you can play what-if with any of the inputs and see the corresponding results.

What if the cost of Google ads went up by 50 percent?

What if the salespeople could close 25 percent more accounts than we thought?

What if they close 25 percent fewer accounts?

What if I spend more on advertising?

Having a working financial model gives you the ability to answer all of these questions and countless more.

Let's walk through a few simple examples with the Dollar Cave Club model (as a reminder, you can find it at leversbook.com/ DollarCaveClubModel). If you have your sample model open, follow along with me here.

We will start with the tab labeled "Annual Cash Flow" since cash is so important to an early-stage company. Note that the ending cash balance at the end of the fifth year (2024) is about $500,000. We will use this as a baseline, then start to look at the impact on cash at the end of five years for different scenarios.

To make things easier to visualize, once you have the file open, go up to the Window Menu and select "New Window."[7] That will open a second window into the same file. By default, it will also be on the same tab, although I suggest you select the "Assumptions" tab in the new window and then resize the two windows so you can see the "Assumptions" tab in one window as well as the "Annual Cash Flow" in another window. Now, as we make changes to the "Assumptions" tab, you will instantly

---

7    Note that I'm assuming you're using Microsoft Excel for creating the model, which I strongly encourage you to do.

see the results in the "Annual Cash Flow" tab without having to select different windows or tabs. Effectively, you're getting two views into the same model at the same time.

## WHAT IF WE INCREASED PRICE?

Let's start with something simple. We have an assumption that the monthly subscription price is $29.99. If we were to raise that by roughly 33 percent to $39.99, what do you think will happen to cash? How much more will you have at the end of year five? Think critically about this before trying it in the model.

Many people guess that cash at the end of year five will increase by about 33 percent, but they are wrong.

Let's look at the model to find out why.

In the model, the COGS is proportional to the price we charge. So if the price went up 33 percent, the cost of the products we put in the box would also go up. The contribution margin for the subscription box would stay at a constant 25 percent. But what about cash?

If your document is open, go ahead and type "$39.99" for the monthly subscription price on the "Assumptions" tab.

You now have $1,205,822 at the end of year five instead of a 33 percent increase from the base scenario, which was a 140 percent increase.

Were you surprised by how much your cash at the end of the five years jumped? How did that happen?

Before I explain how it happened, I want to pause and make an important point: If you were not able to accurately predict how one simple price change in a simple subscription business would impact cash (note that *nothing* else changed here) without referring to the financial model, then how will you be able to predict the impact on your business when you make bigger decisions? Without being able to predict the impact of decisions accurately, what are you using to make these decisions? Without a financial model, you are effectively driving the car without the ability to see out the windshield.

So what did happen here? How did a 33 percent increase in price result in a 140 percent increase in cash? This goes back to the reason we formatted the income statement as we did.[8]

Remember how we grouped revenue and COGS to calculate gross profit? Here is why. When we increased the subscription price, both the revenue and the gross profit from the subscription portion of the business increased by 33 percent. But all of the indirect costs and all of the sales and marketing costs stayed the same. Before we raised the price, we had a lower gross profit and there was just enough money to pay for sales and marketing and indirect costs, which left us with $500K in cash at the end of five years.

But when the price was increased and gross profit increased, every dollar of incremental gross profit went to the bottom line (since all expenses were covered already) and landed in your bank account. If you understand this, you understand that the amount of cash on hand is not related to the percentage increase

---

8    The formatting of the income statement does not change the bottom line, but how you group the expenses and subtotals does affect your ability to understand how you get there.

in price or in gross profit but rather in the *absolute additional dollars of gross profit generated.*

## IF YOU CHANGE ONE ASSUMPTION, REVISIT THE OTHERS

Now, it is not fair to believe that we can raise a price without impacting the customer's willingness to pay. I will use churn to be a proxy for the customer's willingness to pay. So if I increased price by 33 percent, I may guess that churn will increase by 33 percent also.

Let's try that out. Go to the "Assumptions" tab and increase the "Monthly Subscription Churn" from 4 percent to 5.33 percent (a 33 percent increase). Before you look, try to predict what the impact of the increased churn will be. Will you be back to $500K of cash in year five? Lower? Higher? Take an educated guess, then enter the number.

Your ending cash balance in year five is now $860,011—you're still way ahead.

It is counterintuitive, but if you raise prices 33 percent and that in turn increases churn by 33 percent, you have more money in the bank. What rate would churn have to increase to in order for the price increase to be offset just enough so you have the same $500K in the bank at the end of year five? You can start testing, either by entering different values into the churn assumption or by using the Goal Seek function on the tools menu of Excel. You will see that the breakeven point is about 7.3 percent churn.

Armed with that information, you can go out and execute a test with real customers. Increase the price to $39.99/month and if churn is below 7.3 percent per month, the test is a success and you should increase your pricing. If the churn is greater than 7.3 percent, the test is a failure and you shouldn't increase your pricing.

In other words, you now have a way to combine financial modeling with real customer data to predict the future.

## RUNNING MORE WHAT-IF SCENARIOS TO FIND THE LEVERS THAT MATTER

Clearly, we can continue to do this sort of what-if exercise with any of the assumptions in the model. I strongly suggest that after each time you adjust assumptions, you go back to the "base case" where the model was when you first opened it. Let's do that now: return the subscription price to $29.99 and churn to 4 percent—that is the base case, and you can start to look at the impact of other levers you can pull.

Some levers make very little difference in the business, such as the block of three assumptions around selling advertising on the site—page view per visit, cost per thousand (CPM) growth, and MAX CPM charged. There is nothing reasonable you can do to these assumptions that will get you to have meaningful impact on cash. But this is great news! It means that you should spend *zero* cycles trying to sell advertising on your site and can instead take all those resources and put them behind something that will matter.

In the real world, I would zero out those three assumptions and anything else to do with selling advertising, but since we want to maintain the base case as reference, leave them as they were.

## WHAT IF WE SPENT MORE ON ADVERTISING?

Now, what impact do you think spending more on advertising will have? Before you answer (and before you cheat by just changing the assumption), try to think about what you would need to know to answer the question.

You might want to explore the "Unit Economics" tab in the model before trying to answer. As you dig in there, you will see that a dollar spent does indeed return more than a dollar in gross profit but that it takes time. Some people may think it takes too much time. If you are trying to optimize for cash on hand in year five, do you want to spend more in customer acquisition or not?

Now that you have thought about it, go to the "Assumptions" tab and update the assumption labeled "Monthly SEM Spend" (Google Ads). In the default model, the monthly SEM spend is tied to the Facebook spend just to make things simpler. So if you change the SEM spend, the Facebook spend will automatically change with it.

What happens when you double the spend to $20,000 each?

Ending cash balance in year five increases from $500K to $1.1M.

If that was good, what about doubling it again to $40,000 each?

You now have $2.3M in year five. That quadrupled your cash on hand.

But, wait, do you see the problem? Look carefully. Spending $40,000/month on Facebook and Google ended up sending you into bankruptcy in year one. You did not survive long enough to see that great result in year five.

There are a number of ways to solve for this problem. The most realistic would be to make marketing spend a function of revenue and cash on hand. It does not make sense that a company would spend the same amount of money on marketing in its sixth month as it would in its sixtieth. You could write a formula for the marketing spend that takes both into account, spending more as revenue grows but never spending more than 30 percent of the cash on hand, for example. This would protect you from spending more than you have and allow you to increase your growth rate.

But how else can we solve for running out of money? If you look at row twenty-two on the "Annual Cash Flow" tab, you will see "Equity Financing"—so why not just raise more money?

## WHAT IF WE RAISED MORE MONEY?

If we raised $1.5M instead of $1.0M in the first round, we would certainly have enough to bring the marketing spend up to $40,000 and still have a cash buffer. As the founder of Dollar Cave Club, do you want to raise 50 percent more capital in the first round and increase marketing spend, or keep the status quo as it was at $10,000/month and keep the equity?

I have built both an assumption for fundraising ("Raise at Month 1" on the "Assumptions" tab) and an entire tab for visualizing your equity value ("Charts"). Now that you understand how to use the model, look at all three charts on the "Charts" tab. The first one is revenue and expenses, the second is cash on hand, and the third approximates the founders' portion of the equity over time. See how each changes as you increase the marketing spend, and then increase the money raised in the first month from $1M to $1.5M. Most people are surprised by the outcome.

Yes, you are selling 50 percent more of the business, but that does not mean you have 50 percent less of the business. (Read that again—it is not a mistake!) You see, when you raised $1M on a $3M pre-money valuation in the base case, the post-money valuation was $4M and the investors owned 25 percent of the business.[9] The rest (75 percent) was divided up between founders and stock options for employees. If instead you raise $1.5M with the same $3M pre-money valuation, the post-money valuation is now $4.5M and the investors own 33 percent of the business and 67 percent is held by the founders and stock options for employees.

In the scenario where you raise 50 percent more capital, you have the resources to spend 4x on marketing, resulting in almost double the revenue in year five and four times the cash on hand. And your portion of the company only went down from 75 percent to 67 percent after the first raise. A small amount of dilution for a large increase in the company's value.

---

9   Pre-money valuation is simply the valuation (or price) the investors are setting on the company *before* the new investment is made. The post-money valuation is the valuation after the investment is made, and you can calculate it by adding the pre-money valuation plus the new cash invested.

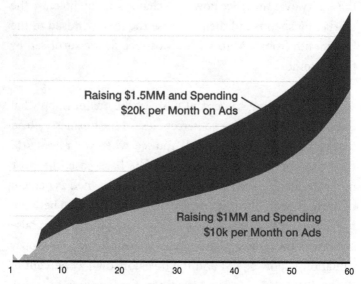

Raising $1.5MM and Spending
$20k per Month on Ads

Raising $1MM and Spending
$10k per Month on Ads

1   10   20   30   40   50   60

Figure 5.10: Founder's Equity Value, Raising $1M and Spending $10K per Month on Advertising

If you do not fully understand this last what-if scenario, I strongly suggest you go back and reread it, play with the model, look at the "Charts" tab, and make sure you can see it in action. Too many entrepreneurs make decisions about how much to raise based on gut feel and not facts and numbers. This model is a solution.

The Dollar Cave Club model is there for you to experiment with and learn how powerful a model can be for predicting your future and help you make better decisions.

## UPDATING THE MODEL REGULARLY

Working with the Dollar Cave Club model is interesting, but once you have a model for your business, how do you use it to make *you* a better operator and run *your* business better? The key comes not only in updating the model regularly (every month) but also in how you update it.

At the end of each month, you should duplicate your latest version of the model and rename the new one with the current date. Next, take your model and start tweaking the assumptions to make the numbers for the month you just completed and look close to what actually happened. Almost every assumption will have to be updated, even if just a little bit.

Once you get it all close enough, leave the newly adjusted assumptions where they are. Go into the columns for the latest closed month and update the data with actual numbers from your accounting system by hard coding or replacing the formulas with actual numbers you type in. Then shade that column to indicate that it contains actual numbers and they will never change (since they represent the past that has already happened).

If you look at the sample for Dollar Cave Club, you will see that I have done this through May of 2020. If you consistently update your model each month this way, the assumptions will get more and more accurate, and it will predict the future better and better each month. It really is like having a crystal ball and being able to see the future.

## USING THE FINANCIAL MODEL TO FUNDRAISE

I already told you the story of how every investor who spent the time to sit down with me and review the financial model for SurePayroll either invested in the company or offered to invest and we turned them down. So how did we accomplish that?

To be fair, there was selection bias in the group. They would not have invested the time to review the model with me if they were not already interested. With that said, here is what I did.

In the fundraising deck, I had a "teaser" of the financials—a single slide with only a handful of rows (revenue, COGS, sales and marketing, general and administrative expenses [G&A], earnings before interest, taxes, depreciation, and amortization [EBITDA]) for the next five years. I would spend enough time on that slide that they would inevitably ask a question such as, "What is the basis for that revenue growth?" or "Why is X growing faster than Y?" and that was when I knew they took the bait. So I set the hook.

I responded with, "It all comes out of the detailed five-year model that we have developed," and I would pause. After five to ten seconds, almost everyone would ask for the model, and I would respond with a very surprising no.

Okay, so I was more polite than that. I would explain that I really wanted to make the process as easy as possible for them and that I would like to schedule ninety minutes with them and an associate to review the model. I assured them that after reviewing it with them, I would leave them a copy. They inevitably said, "Oh, just send it over. We are good with models."

But I had two objectives here that both required a meeting:

1. I want to make the model easy for them to understand and not frustrating at all. The best way I know to do that is to walk them through it, explaining along the way and fielding any questions they had before they became frustrated.
2. Raising money is about building relationships. Any opportunity to get more face time with a potential investor was

going to increase the strength of the relationship and the likelihood that they would invest.

So when they said to "just send it over," I would push back and explain, "I want to make it as easy for you as possible, and sitting down with you and an associate for ninety minutes will ensure that you get your questions answered and understand the model as quickly as possible. Do you have time Thursday, or is next Tuesday better?"

I held my ground and always got the next meeting.

The second part of the trick is how you manage the review of the financial model. First, always make a copy of your most current model and give it a file name that includes the investor and date. That way, you can make changes in "Assumptions" while working with that investor, save the file, and have an exact copy of what you talked about to send the investor and to keep in your files.

Now that you have a fresh copy ready to review with the investor, you have to be sure to set expectations properly. After the perfunctory greetings, I always start by thanking them for making time. Then I tell them, "Before we get started, I want you to know that the only thing I know for sure about this model is that it is wrong."

That set the tone for us to be working together, sitting side by side, us against the model to test and challenge it (not me). If they thought assumptions were wrong, I would update the model with their assumptions and show them the results. To do this deftly requires that *you* have a command of the model— likely that you have built it yourself. For example, you know that if an investor were looking at Dollar Cave Club and wanted to change assumptions on advertising revenue, you could change almost anything and it would not matter. If they thought churn was going to be 8 percent, then you know you should push back as that is a losing proposition.

At the end of the meeting, I would save a copy of the file we were working on with their name and date and then send it to them to play with. By that time, they hopefully thought I had a great handle on what drives the business, and they understood the handful of things that were risks to the business and were confident that we could tackle them. It worked.

## NOW IT'S YOUR TURN

A financial model can be used to better manage your business, help you construct tests, inform better decisions, and replace your gut with data in decision making. It can also help you be more efficient in raising money, both in understanding how much you need to raise and the impact of raising more or less, if you choose to pursue that route.

When you combine the financial model with the rest of the tools in this book, you can begin to move into true repeatability into your business. Rather than just relying on blind intuition or guesswork, you will have an actual data-driven model that will allow you to move your business at the speed of your own ambition.

## CHAPTER 6

# NOW WHAT?

## (BY AMOS SCHWARTZFARB AND TREVOR BOEHM)

First of all, congratulations! If you are here, that means you've gone through all the exercises in this book and have built a data-driven model that you understand and believe in deeply.

If you've done the work outlined here, you've probably spent at least twenty to forty hours working on your business, not counting the time it took to read. Maybe you have a ton of new insights, or maybe you've just taken what you already knew and organized and formalized it. In any case, you've done a ton of hard work, and that is a great start.

But what do you do with it all? How do you turn all this work into a business that is repeatable and can grow? The great news is, you now have everything you need to create a plan to transition from working *on* your business to working *in* your business.

## CREATING YOUR PLAN

Your model is essentially your plan. The financial model represents the mechanics of your business, and by plugging in different assumptions (and revising each month), you are creating (and re-creating) your plan.

Now you need to actually formalize the plan. In other words, "Who does what by when?" Take the elements of the levers you have identified and assign an owner. Because you all built the plan together, you should already be in alignment on *what* needs to get done. Now it's up to each person to become responsible for their area and figure out *how* to get it done.

### ASSIGN OWNERS FOR EACH LEVER

As a leadership team, assign who's responsible for each of the levers you've identified in your business. For example, go back through the revenue drivers and subdrivers in your financial model and ask yourselves, who owns each of these drivers? Who is responsible for executing on the activities that get you to those outputs? Similarly, as you look through your KPIs, which team is responsible for tracking and reporting on those metrics? What is their plan for ensuring your actual progress reflects what you want to see in the business? Each team member should clearly know their area of responsibility, the KPIs they will measure to know that they are on track, as well as how their work ties back to a value or values in your revenue formula and, ultimately, financial model.

### WORK WITH EACH OWNER TO CREATE THEIR PLAN

Next, each team member can go make their own plan. How is each team going to execute based on the financial model to reach the goals you've laid out for yourself? As a leader, you will work with each of those teams to make sure they have a clear and believable plan to execute on what you have collectively modeled. Then come back as a group and make sure that there is still alignment. And maybe most importantly, the CEO (or president or owner or whoever is ultimately responsible for running the business) needs to believe in every aspect of the plan.

We'd like to say that's it, but as we're sure you already know, it's not nearly that easy. Even after the hard work identifying and testing the levers that now make up your model, the only thing you can know for sure is that it's (at least a little) wrong. You're not trying to get it exactly right anyway because the real goal isn't to be right 100 percent of the time. Instead, you want to expand your region of what you can predict and control in the business. The work you did in this book is intended to be the foundation that you'll continue to iterate on for the rest of the life of the business.

In other words, it's always going to be hard work to build a long-term sustainable business.

### REGULARLY SHARE AND REVIEW YOUR PROGRESS

As a company, you should be getting together *weekly* to share your progress in the form of metrics and data that show how you are moving your responsibilities forward. Anecdotal information and storytelling is fine to support the data but should not be the core of "how you did this week."

As a leadership team, you should be getting together every quarter to redo all the work in this book. Yep, you read that correctly: every three months, you should talk about your W3 and revenue formula, your validated and unvalidated assumptions, your KPIs, and a revision of your financial model. The great news here is that every single time you do this, it'll become quicker and more refined, and as a team, you will get more and more aligned. The first few quarters could take a similar amount of time, but within a few quarters, expect that the time will be cut to one-fourth or less of what it took to get started.

There you have it. You now have a five-step process to building repeatability into your business so that you can understand and control your own destiny.

Good luck on your journey! If you want to give us feedback, let us know how the process is working for you, or if you're interested in working with us directly, check us out at www.leversbook.com.

AMOS, TREVOR, CODY, AND TROY

# APPENDIX

## THE SIXTH QUESTION: WHY DO YOU EXIST?

### (BY CODY SIMMS)

This book is about bringing data and model-based thinking into every part of your business. But to make any use of that data, there is one critical element that you need first:

A reason to exist.

This isn't a wild, existential question like "Why are we all here?" It's the reason you are building your business in the first place. Why did you decide to take the long and lonely road to building a business? Why do you wake up every morning and get out of bed? How do you want to impact the world, or your community, or whomever it is that you intend to bring value to?

We wrestled with whether to include this section in the book. Unlike the other chapters, this is about a question that is fundamentally *untestable*. It boils down to what you believe should be true about the world. Yet, as different from the others as it is, a company's fundamental why is critical for creating alignment and direction for any team. Having an unclear purpose will make the work you do through this book (whether solo or with your team) much harder.

So we decided to include a simple exercise in creating a cultural mission statement that Cody adapted from master design leader Dave Holland here in the Appendix. If you already have an explicit and articulate mission your team is working on, you can use this as an exercise in further exploring that mission. If you don't have one, we hope this gets you to a working version that can guide your work through the rest of the book.

Whenever you're ready, go grab your team, stock a room with some food and water, lock the door, and let's get to work.

## HOW TO GET TO THE HEART OF YOUR PURPOSE

Here is how it's going to work. We're going to start with a few "conversational statements" designed to get you all thinking and talking about the team, the work you do, and why you do it. Then, once you've all agreed on that set of statements, we'll use them as fodder for creating a full mission statement. Depending on your current level of internal alignment and clarity as a team, this can take you anywhere from a couple of hours to forever. So if you get stuck after two hours, don't be afraid to take a break and come back to it.

The statements that you create may still need some wordsmithing over time, but that's a different level of work that we don't need to worry too much about right now. For the purposes of this book, the wording does not need to be perfect; it just needs to be something everyone on the core team is aligned on. That way, as you get into the meaty work later on in this book, everyone will be working from common goals.

CONVERSATIONAL STATEMENTS

1. "We are…"
2. "We do…"
3. "We believe…"

Let's flesh out what these mean.

- The **We Are** statement: Who are we as a team? How do we refer to ourselves and people like us? As you craft the statement, think about whom you believe your customers are and your connection between your customers and you. Your "We are…" statement is not about your product. It's about the inclusive commonality that makes up all of your people collectively and shows up across your company.
- The **We Do** statement: What job do we do for our customers? This is literally a statement of what you do for your customers. It's the job you perform for your customers, and it's thought of more tactically than the other statements. You can swap the verb *do* for something more active or descriptive of the actions you take.
- The **We Believe** statement: What beliefs drive us? As you craft the statement, think about why your customers care about what you do and why you care about helping your customers.

Answer each question one at a time by yourself. After every person answers a question, get back together and talk about each answer. Comment on each other's answers and call out things you like and don't like. Write down the words and phrases from each that you like and keep track of them. Then move on to the next question and do it all again.

Once you're aligned on your statements, you can stitch them together into one overarching sentence:

"We are...who...because..."

Seeing the sentence come together can be satisfying, but don't focus too much on getting that exact sentence right. What matters most are the handful of words and phrases that stuck out to you and that you want to remember. You'll use these as the foundation for the next step: your purpose and vision statements.

## PURPOSE AND VISION STATEMENTS

1. Our Purpose (why we exist):
2. Our Vision (aspiration):

With the conversational positioning statements you just created and the bank of words and phrases that you found while creating them, it's time to start the work of drafting the actual cultural mission statement. You can break the cultural mission statement into two parts:

- **Your Purpose (why you exist):** Now think broadly. What is *the thing* your company is on this earth to do? What is your base, core purpose for being—boiled down to its most essential element(s)?
- **Your Vision (aspiration):** For this part, be aspirational—if you are wildly successful, how will the world have changed? What paradigm shift does your business bring at scale? This

is the kind of impact that is so aspirational that you will probably never reach it, but you want it to inform everything your company does.

We define an effective mission statement as a combination of purpose and vision. It's the most core element of why you exist (purpose) combined with what will happen if you are wildly successful (vision), and together, that is the mission you are on every day: "We do X to have a chance to achieve a grandiose Y."

The original mission statements of two of the largest tech companies in the world show how effective this structure can be in communicating a company's reason for being.

### Google's Mission Statement

*To organize the world's information and make it universally accessible and useful.*

Google's mission statement is perhaps the best at doing this, and no surprise, Google has been one of the most successful and iconic companies of the twenty-first century thus far. Google's mission: "To organize the world's information and make it universally accessible and useful." Let's break that down. Their purpose is the first part of the statement: "To organize the world's information." It is *the thing that Google is on earth to do*. Google's parent company, Alphabet, today has many different product offerings and services that stray from this purpose, but if you look at the things inside the Google product suite, almost everything there—from search to Gmail to Docs and more— fits pretty squarely in this purpose. And the second part of the statement is, to "make it universally accessible and useful." This is the aspirational piece. It's pretty clearly impossible to make the world's information universally accessible and useful, but that's their ultimate goal and drives their activities. It gives the company a sense of aspiration, and together, their purpose and their aspiration drive their mission. It's hard to argue with their results.

### Facebook's (Original) Mission Statement

Facebook changed their mission statement in 2017. But let's look at their original mission statement—the one that drove them through one of the most impressive growth curves in the history of business and allowed them to achieve what at the time was the largest IPO in history. Their original mission statement is also a great encapsulation of purpose + aspirational vision: "To give people the power to share and make the world more open and connected." Purpose: "To give people the power to share"—it's hard to argue that this wasn't what Facebook was on earth to do from its founding in 2004 through 2017. And its aspirational vision was to "make the world more open and connected." One could argue whether Facebook has successfully achieved this vision—and perhaps this is a reason for the rearticulation in 2017—but it certainly gave the company something to aim for.

So now it's your turn to give this a try for your company. As you do, keep in mind, there are NO wrong answers here *as long as you and your core team are aligned.*

You are free to interpret these questions however you want. Answer the question however it strikes you, and let each member of your team do the same. The magic in this exercise lies in your coming together, with sometimes very different answers, and then working together on creating a unified statement.

## PUTTING IT ALL TOGETHER

When working on this book, we did this exercise exactly how I'm describing it to you (and we did it over Zoom). Sometimes our answers were similar and sometimes very different. This is where we landed:

1. Who **we are**: Business builders
2. What **we do**: Get growing companies to repeatable revenue
3. Why **we believe** it matters: Every entrepreneur should be equipped to control their own destiny

Our cultural mission statement:

1. **What's our purpose (why we exist):** To equip all business builders to find and move their levers of control...
2. **Vision (aspiration):** ...and build the world they imagine.

Here's what it looks like all together:

> We are business builders who enable growing companies to build repeatable revenue in their business because we believe that every entrepreneur should be equipped to control their own destiny.

> We exist to equip all business builders to find and move their levers of control and build the world they imagine.

The collective answers to those questions turned into very clear statements of why we exist, for whom, and to what purpose. Because we did this together, we are all aligned.

As our reader—our target "customer" for this mission—you will either identify (or not) with our statements. If you do, hopefully you found a ton of very actionable value in the rest of the book.

# AMOS'S ACKNOWLEDGMENTS

I always enjoy writing this part because I get to tell people thank you for helping me and supporting me (even if I didn't in real time and even if you didn't know).

First to my family: To my wife, Roseann, for continuing to support my crazy and my ability to always take on more than I should at any given time. And to my daughters, Sierra and Callie, who are the driving force for everything I do professionally. I love you all so much.

Next, I want to thank my co-author, Trevor, as well as Cody and Troy, who have contributed so much to this book. It's been amazing to bring all our work together, and I'm so thankful and appreciative of your friendships.

I also want to thank Haley Bohem, CEO of SkillPop, Meggie Williams, CEO of Skipper, Char Hu, CEO of The Helper Bees, Monica Landers, CEO of Authors.me, Katy Aucoin, CEO of DearDuck, Hersh Tapadia, CEO of Allstacks, Brooke Bains, CEO of Bombshell, David Bain, Bain Realty, Chris Riply, CEO of Smartersorting, Kurt Rathmann, Noah Spirakus, Dan Green, and all the other founders who've provided great feedback along the way.

It's also important to me to thank Jake Winebaum, Brian Barnum, Dan Machock, Kevin Gaither, and Zoe Schlag who have been pivotal in helping to build my foundation of knowledge and experience.

Finally, I have to call out the music that helped get me through both the writing and editing. As usual, I listened to a lot of Grateful Dead, and in particular Dick's Picks Volume 16 (11/8/69 from Fillmore Auditorium in San Francisco) while writing and a lot of Red Hot Chili Peppers (particularly *Californication*) while editing. I also started listening to Phish again after almost twenty years, and gosh, they've gotten even better!

# TREVOR'S ACKNOWLEDGMENTS

To my co-conspirators over the years—John Boiles, Zoe Schlag, Mark Hand, Reagan Pugh, and Evan Loomis. Our scars have been the source material for most of the insights in this book.

To the entrepreneurs I've invested in and worked alongside over the years—Albert Santalo, Sadoc Paredes, Feliciano Paredes, Roxana Castro Camargo, Andrea Segato Bertaia, Chen Zhang, Matt Udvari, Cory Siskand, Mike Maniscalco, Bargava Subramanian, Tuhin Sharma, Nikhil Jois, Aaron Hsu, Evan DeGray, Derek Omori, Lauren Tracy, Greta McAnany, Rena Pacheco-Theard, Dan Driscoll, Jamee Herbert, JC Kirst, Karyn Scott, Sera Bonds, Zach House, Alima Bawah, Peter Awin, Felicia Jackson, Matthew Cyr, Chris Gatbonton, Katy Aucoin, Simone Spence, Kwaku Owusu, Melanie Igwe, Jason Fox, Jake Boshernitzan, Caroline Caselli, Dan Green, Shelby Stephens, Zach Fragapane, Dani Cherkassky, Boutaina Faruq, Rameez Hoque, Alejandra Rodriguez Boughton, Ott Jalakas, Mait Muntel, Andrew Gibbs-Dabney, Soga Oni, Genevieve Barnard Oni, Cesar Manduca, Carlos Rosso, Ani Bagepalli, Jerold McDonald, Chris Cummings, Katica Roy, Dan Hnatkovskyy, Sofia Vyshnevska, Ruben Rathnasingham, Laurin Leonard, Teresa Hodge, Emily Williams, Cole Williams, Alison Anderson, Brian Hoang, Virginie Maire, Matthieu Viala, Surbhi Rathore, Toshish Jawale, Bernard Parks, Anna Scott, Yan Azdoud, Chris Kelley, Luke Marshall, Ikpeme Neto, Aaron Welch, Buzz White, Hersh Tapadia, and others. There is no better or more honorable job than to come behind someone who is taking meaningful risk and help make what they believe should be in the world a reality. I'm lucky to be a part of your stories and to call you friends.

To Cody and Troy—I'm honored you agreed to work on this book with us. You've both taught me an immense amount about what it means to be a good operator and a good investor.

To Amos—Thanks for having boldness to imagine this book in the first place and for inviting me on the journey to write it with you. The energy you bring with every company you work with inspires me.

To Candice—You've put up with more than a few crazy endeavors over the years, and I'm deeply grateful. Thank you for all the balls you picked up that I never even saw that I dropped, for the feedback that helps me do better work and become a better person, and most of all, for loving and believing in me. I love you.

# ABOUT THE AUTHORS

## AMOS SCHWARTZFARB

Amos Schwartzfarb has been building businesses for twenty-five years and investing in startups for the past ten. A job packing boxes in 1997 led to his stellar career in startups—helping to start and build businesses that sold to Yahoo!, R. H. Donnelly, The Home Depot, and more. Amos has also spent the last six years as Managing Director of Techstars Austin where he's invested in over one hundred companies. Today, he's a startup advisor, investor, and author of the bestselling book *Sell More Faster: The Ultimate Sales Playbook for Startups*. In his spare time, you can find Amos hanging out with his wife and two kids, riding one of his bikes, or playing music.

## TREVOR BOEHM

Trevor began his career as a writer, working among the immigrant and Native American communities in Texas and Montana, and then found his way into building companies. He is a serial founder and a former Managing Director with Techstars. At Techstars, Trevor led Alexa Next Stage, a program for later-stage startups that was run in partnership with the Amazon Alexa Fund, and he worked on Techstars's first accelerator for mission-driven companies. He is interested in the intersections between personal, team, and company growth, and lives in Austin, Texas, with his wife and two kids.

## TROY HENIKOFF

Troy Henikoff is Managing Director of MATH Venture Partners. Additionally, Troy is an active mentor with Techstars. Troy was a co-founder of Excelerate Labs, which became Techstars Chicago in 2013. He also helps manage the FireStarter Fund, teaches entrepreneurship at Northwestern University's Kellogg School of Business, and is on the board of the Chicagoland Entrepreneurial Center. Prior to Techstars Chicago, Troy was CEO of OneWed.com, President of Amacai, and Co-founder and CEO of SurePayroll.com.

## CODY SIMMS

Cody Simms resides in Los Angeles and is Partner and Senior Vice-President of Investments at Techstars, one of the most active early-stage venture investors in the world. Earlier in his career, Cody held roles including Chief Product Officer at StumbleUpon, Vice-President of Product Management at Yahoo!, and Product Manager at *The New York Times*, Sprint, and NBC Internet/Snap.com. Cody has recently co-founded Climate Changemakers, a nonpartisan, nationwide, community-driven movement to channel climate concern into climate action.